G000229282

100
HISTORY
LESSONS

- Inspirational ideas
- Step-by-step guidance
- Photocopiable resources

AGES
5-7

Paul Bowen and
Pat Hoodless

CREDITS

Authors
Paul Bowen
Pat Hoodless

Illustrations
Jane Bottomley

Editor
Victoria Lee

Series Designer
Joy Monkhouse

Assistant Editor
Catherine Gilhooly

Designer
Erik Ivens

Text © 2006 Paul Bowen
and Pat Hoodless
© 2006 Scholastic Ltd

Designed using Adobe InDesign

Published by Scholastic Ltd
Villiers House
Clarendon Avenue
Leamington Spa
Warwickshire CV32 5PR

www.scholastic.co.uk

Printed by Bell and Bain Ltd, Glasgow

123456789   6789012345

British Library Cataloguing-in-Publication Data
A catalogue record for this book is available from the British Library.

ISBN 0-439-96499-7
ISBN 978-0439-96499-9

ACKNOWLEDGEMENTS

Rosica Colin Limited for use of 'Bombardment' by Richard Aldington from *Collected Poems 1905–1925* by Richard Aldington © 1971, The Estate of Richard Aldington (1971, Scholarly Press).
The Royal Engineers Library for the use of an extract from George Smith's diary © The Royal Engineers Library, Chatham.
John West for the use of an extract from *Tell Tale 4: Victorian Britain* by John West © 1990, John West (1990, ELM Publications).

Extracts from The National Literacy Strategy and The National Numeracy Strategy © Crown copyright. Reproduced under the terms of HMSO Guidance Note 8.

Extracts from Programmes of Study from The National Curriculum reproduced under the terms of HMSO Guidance Note 8. © Qualifications and Curriculum Authority.

Extracts from QCA Innovating with History © Qualifications and Curriculum Authority.

Every effort has been made to trace copyright holders and the publishers apologise for any inadvertent omissions.

Due to the nature of the web, we cannot gurantee the content or links of any of the sites featured. We strongly recommend that teachers check websites before using them in the classroom.

Contents

100 HISTORY LESSONS: AGES 5-7

100 History Lessons: Ages 5-7 provides a series of lessons which build upon the QCA Schemes of Work for History at Key Stage 1. It contains eight chapters, each one focusing on a key study unit from the Scheme of Work, including the newer adapted study units:

1. Toys
2. Homes
3. Castles
4. Seaside holidays
5. Florence Nightingale
6. Isambard Kingdom Brunel
7. The Great Fire of London
8. Remembrance Day.

History skills and concepts

A key focus of the lessons provided in this book is the development of historical skills and concepts through appropriate and enjoyable activities. The key skills and concepts that are required in the *National Curriculum for History in England and Wales* and which also apply to the Scottish curriculum for history are clearly identified for each lesson.

In order to aid planning, these essential historical skills and concepts are set out at the beginning of each chapter in a grid. These grids show at a glance how the topics, skills and concepts are mapped out through the book and give links to key historical objectives for each lesson.

EXAMPLE taken from 'Castles'

OBJECTIVES	MAIN ACTIVITY
To communicate their learning about castles through role play. To apply their knowledge and understanding of life in a castle a long time ago.	A Great Hall is created and children role play life in a castle in the past, taking the parts of lords, ladies, servants, cooks and soldiers.
To find out about the past from written sources. To apply their knowledge and understanding of life in a castle a long time ago.	Children learn about food eaten in castles in the past. They look at an example of a medieval menu and then create a menu for the role-play area.

Lesson plans

In addition to listing key objectives for every activity, each lesson plan also outlines how to approach each activity, the resources that it requires, any information to guide preparation for teaching the lesson and guidance on assessment and how this relates to further planning.

Concise background information which you may need to support your teaching of the lesson is also provided. Activities are sequenced and can be used as a whole unit of work, or they can be selected and used within your own existing scheme of work. Many of the lesson activities are accompanied by photocopiable sheets; these are clearly identified in the grids with the symbol 🄿 .

Differentiation

Each lesson plan includes suggested ways of differentiating activities for lower abilities and the more able children in a year group. Plans also discuss how lessons can be adapted for use with a different age group or for a wide age range within a mixed age class.

History and the wider curriculum

The lessons in this book are particularly focused towards fostering and developing creativity, especially through links made across the curriculum. History is an excellent vehicle through which to enrich the wider curriculum and in particular through its natural links with literacy, geography, ICT and citizenship. It provides children with great opportunities to:
● refine their communication and information-processing skills in a range of contexts
● develop and extend their investigative and problem-solving skills, including using number and ICT, inside and outside the classroom
● participate in a range of independent and collaborative learning experiences, which extend their personal, social and study skills
● gain experiences that help them to make connections between themselves, their communities and the wider world
● develop awareness and understanding of a range of peoples and cultures and a respect for many different attitudes, views and beliefs
● recognise the need for a just and equitable society and their own role in making this possible
● explore current issues within an historical context to make sense of the world around them and develop the skills and attitudes necessary for active involvement as citizens.
(QCA, Innovating with History, www.qca.org.uk/history/innovating/ wider_curriculum.htm)

A key feature of this book therefore are the links it makes with other curriculum areas, in particular literacy, numeracy and ICT. In keeping with the Primary Strategy, the chapters in this book that particularly make the connection with other areas of the curriculum are those that build upon the new QCA Schemes of Work. These units make use of cross-curricular links in adapting existing units or combining them with units of work from other subject areas. They are, at Key Stage 1, the units on Castles, Seaside holidays and Isambard Kingdom Brunel (see the QCA Innovating with History website found on www.qca.org.uk/ history).

Geography features prominently, since at Key Stage 1 there is an emphasis on making use of the children's own locality and school, more distant localities, and on introducing the notion of maps, plans and globes. Art, design and technology are areas widely used throughout the lessons, as a means of encouraging a creative response to learning and sometimes as an assessment opportunity. Drama is a part of the National Curriculum for English, which can enhance a history lesson and bring it to life. Through simulation and role play children have the opportunity to obtain first-hand experience of the feelings and emotions of people in past situations. The development of Speaking and Listening skills are a central feature of many of the lesson plans.

CHAPTER 1

Toys

This chapter supports Unit 1 'How are our toys different from those in the past?' in the QCA Scheme of Work for History. Through engaging and stimulating lessons, the children will develop skills in observation and sorting to gain a sense of chronology, as well as learn appropriate vocabulary to describe old and new toys.

The children will be encouraged to study primary sources, such as artefacts, as well as secondary sources in the form of information books. Some advance preparation will be needed, especially in collecting old and new toys. It will be useful to contact local history museums as some may offer support in providing suitable artefacts.

	OBJECTIVES	MAIN ACTIVITY
Lesson 1	To find out about the past from objects.	Children create displays of old and new toys, noting differences and drawing an example.
Lesson 2 Ⓟ	To place objects in chronological order. To use common words and phrases relating to the passing of time.	Children sort toys in a variety of ways, then sort pictures of toys into sets of old and new, using the photocopiable sheet.
Lesson 3 Ⓟ	To use common words and phrases relating to the passing of time. To understand the difference between old and new.	Children develop vocabulary to describe old-fashioned toys and then match words to pictures on the photocopiable sheet.
Lesson 4 Ⓟ	To develop historical vocabulary. To use everyday words and phrases to describe artefacts.	Children discuss features of old-fashioned toys as a whole class and in pairs, then draw and write about a toy on their own.
Lesson 5	To use oral sources to find out about the past.	In pairs, children talk about and draw their favourite toys.
Lesson 6	To find out about the past from first-hand experience of old-fashioned games.	Children take part in an old-fashioned PE lesson, using 'drill' exercises and old-fashioned toys.
Lesson 7 Ⓟ	To find out about the past by making old-fashioned toys.	Children make old-fashioned paper doll puppets.
Lesson 8 Ⓟ	To find out about the past from poems. To extend vocabulary by using words linked to a topic.	As a class, children listen to a poem written in the past, talk about it and create a new story or poem about a toy in the class collection.
Lesson 9 Ⓟ	To find out about the past from pictures and photographs.	In pairs, children identify old-fashioned features in pictures. On their own, they cut out pictures of old-fashioned toys to complete a family scene.
Lesson 10	To communicate their knowledge of history in a variety of ways.	Individually or in pairs, the children label historical features on a copy of an old photograph.
Lesson 11	To communicate their knowledge of history in a variety of ways.	Children work in groups to create a toyshop: preparing the shop banner, making labels, sorting out money and arranging toys.
Lesson 12	To communicate their knowledge of history in a variety of ways.	Children make a timeline, sequencing toys in chronological order and producing information, in pairs, to go with the exhibits.

Collecting toys

Objectives
● To find out about the past from objects.

Vocabulary
toy, old, new

Resources
Large sheets of drawing paper; coloured pencils; selection of old and new toys (ask the children to bring in a favourite toy for the display and also museum loan collections are useful sources, along with purchases from museum shops, antique fairs and so on - this collection can be used for further lessons about toys and history).

Background
Toys are an obvious way of engaging the interest of children in the study of the past. Toys are real and meaningful to young children who can easily identify with them, especially if some of their own toys are included. This lesson makes use of children's own experiences as a basis for their learning about children's experiences in the past. In turn, this will help them to develop an understanding of what life was like for children in the past.

Introduction
● Arrange all the toys at the front of the class and explain to the children that they are going to help make a display, or collection, of the toys that have been brought in.
● Talk about the different toys that have been collected, asking, for example: *Which toys do you play with yourselves? Which toys were played with by an older person, such as your parents or grandparents? What are the toys made of - which are plastic and which are made of wood or other materials?*

Main teaching activity
● Help the children to make two displays: one of old toys and one of new toys.
● Discuss and describe the differences between the toys as they are working. Ask them: *How are the toys different and how you can tell?*
● Talk about what materials the different toys are made from, for example, old toys are made of wood and new toys are made of plastic.
● When the displays are completed, give out the drawing paper and pencils and ask the children to draw the toy that they like the best or find most interesting.
● Encourage the children to work independently to produce accurate observational drawings of their selected toy.

Plenary
● Look at the children's pictures with the whole class and review their key features.
● Help the children to sort the drawings into two sets - old and new.
● The pictures could be displayed in these sets on the wall or as 'washing lines' across the classroom.

Links
● NLS Y1-2 Word level work: vocabulary extension by using words linked to a particular topic.
● NC Art and design KS1: (1a) to record from first-hand observation.

Differentiation
Less able children will need support with adding detail to their drawings and in talking about their picture at the end of the lesson. More able children and those in an older age group will be able to write labels or captions for their pictures.

Sorting toys

Objectives
● To place objects in chronological order.
● To use common words and phrases relating to the passing of time.

Vocabulary
older, oldest, newer, newest

Resources
Collection of old and new toys (see page 7); two large hoops or paper circles; the photocopiable sheet 'Sorting toys' on page 19, one per child.

Links
● NNS Y1-2: to solve a given problem by sorting, classifying and organising information in simple ways.
● NC Mathematics KS1: Ma3 (4a) to order objects by direct comparison using appropriate language.
● QCA ICT: Unit 1D 'Labelling and classifying'.

Background
The children learn to group an assortment of toys into two sets. It is helpful to let the children decide their own criteria for sorting the toys at the beginning of the lesson. They can group the toys by size, material, or type, for example. They may choose a variety of categories at first, but in the course of the lesson, you can begin to discuss their ideas and encourage them to categorise the toys according to age. Once the children have gained experience of sorting, they will begin to understand more clearly the concept of sorting the toys according to whether they are 'old' or 'new' - that is, sequencing chronologically.

Introduction
● Lay out on the floor two large hoops or circles of paper into which the toys can be placed.
● Explain to the children that they are going to sort the class collection of toys into two groups.

Main teaching activity
● Show the children one example of how a few of the toys could be sorted into two groups. Ask why those toys could be in the same group. What is the same about all the toys in the group?
● Encourage the children to think about the different ways in which they can sort the toys. Ask questions, such as: *Which toys can we group together? Can they be grouped by size, colour or shape?*
● Once the children have sorted the toys in a few different ways, lead them to sorting the toys into 'old' and 'new' sets. Ask the children to tell you which are the oldest and the newest toys. How do they know? What can they see that tells them this?
● As an assessment activity, use the photocopiable sheet 'Sorting toys' on page 19 and ask the children to sort the pictures of toys into two sets. They can cut out and stick the pictures in the appropriate hoops or draw lines from the pictures to the hoops. As the children organise their pictures, ask them to explain why they are putting the toys into a particular set.

Plenary
● Working with the whole class, help the children to select toys to make a 3D chronological sequence or timeline of toys at the front of the room.

Differentiation
Additional adult support in thinking about the criteria and sorting activities may be needed for less able children and younger children. The photocopiable sheet could be adapted to include three sets for the more able children: new, old, very old.

Matching old and new

Objectives
● To use common words and phrases relating to the passing of time.
● To understand the difference between old and new.

Vocabulary
different, modern, old-fashioned

Resources
Collection of old and new toys (see page 7); the photocopiable sheet 'Old toys, new toys' on page 20 one per child.

Background
Children's understanding of time and chronology is difficult to assess, since sometimes they may have an early understanding of chronology, but may not know the appropriate vocabulary. This lesson provides an assessment opportunity by combining the use of vocabulary with activities designed to assess children's understanding of the concept of old and new.

Introduction
● Discuss the differences between the toys in the collection with the class. Ask questions such as: *Which are old and which are new? How do we know? How are they different?*

Main teaching activity
● Make pairs of old and new versions of the same toy.
● Ask the children to explain how the new toy is different. Note which children have grasped the concept of old and new and are able to make the correct use of vocabulary.
● Look at pictures or examples of old-fashioned toys, such as wax dolls, tin soldiers or wooden toys. Discuss what they are made of and compare them with most modern toys made of plastic.
● Display descriptive words, such as 'wax', 'wooden', 'tin', and 'plastic'.
● Use the photocopiable sheet 'Old toys, new toys' on page 20 to assess the children's ability to identify old and new toys and to match corresponding vocabulary.
● Discuss the wooden toys. Do the children think they are old or new?
● Demonstrate how to complete the sheet by filling in one example with the whole class working together. Then ask the children to finish the rest of the sheet on their own.
● Observe the children during this activity and ask them to explain why they are matching particular labels to certain pictures in order to assess their real understanding of the task.

Plenary
● Review the children's work and clarify any misconceptions, for example: the children have decided a toy is old, simply because it is dirty or because it looks more worn out than another; it is made from less colourful materials than another, and so on.
● Discuss the children's reasons for deciding whether a toy is old or new.

Links
● NLS Y1-2 Word level work: vocabulary extension by using words linked to a particular topic.

Differentiation
Younger and less able readers will need support in reading the labels during the independent task.

Describing old-fashioned toys

Objectives
● To develop historical vocabulary.
● To use everyday words and phrases to describe artefacts.

Vocabulary
old-fashioned, long ago, worn out

Resources
Collection of old-fashioned toys; pictures and books about toys; the photocopiable sheet 'My old-fashioned toy' on page 21, one per child; coloured pencils.

Background
The 'old' toys used for this activity could be from any period, but for ease of identification, the older the better. Replicas of Victorian and Edwardian toys and books are easy to collect from museum shops, for instance, and are fairly easy for children to identify as being old or old-fashioned.

Introduction
● Look at the toys from the collection carefully with the class. Ask the children to say what they think about them.
● Prompt the children with questions such as: *Would you play with toys like these today? Why not?*
● Ask the children how they can tell that the toys are old-fashioned or from long ago. What words could they use to describe the toys? On the board, make a list of the words the children suggest to describe the toys.

Main teaching activity
● Divide the children into pairs and ask each pair to choose one toy from the 'old toys' display.
● Ask the children to work with their partners to describe the toy.
● Give each child a copy of the photocopiable sheet 'My old-fashioned toy' on page 22 and ask them to draw the toy in detail.
● With support as necessary, they should then complete the simple writing frame copied from the photocopiable sheet, using the words they suggested during the introduction.
● Assist the children in using descriptive language when they are writing their sentences.

Plenary
● Share with the class the children's drawings and any descriptive pieces they have written.
● Display the pictures and draw attention to the way they have used descriptive words and phrases.

Links
● NLS Y1–2 Word level work: vocabulary extension by using words linked to a particular topic.
● NC Art and design KS1: (1a) to record from first-hand observation.

Differentiation
Children who complete their work quickly could use the words collected on the board or in the class wordbank to write a short paragraph about one of the toys. Less able children could make a large painting of their favourite toy as an extension activity.

Talking about old toys

Objectives
● To use oral sources to find out about the past.

Vocabulary
speak, special, favourite

Resources
Old toy from your own past that you can talk about or pictures or video footage of someone talking about their favourite old toy; photograph of yourself as a child; small cards, one for each child; drawing materials.

Background
This lesson personalises old toys by linking them to someone's real childhood. In this way, the children will be able to relate to the past more closely and to see how things have changed or stayed the same by comparing their own favourite toys with those they hear about and see. Undoubtedly, the best way to achieve this learning outcome is to bring in a toy of your own, since the children will identify most readily with the experiences of their teacher. However, if this is not possible, pictures, videos and CDs could be used as an alternative. A useful follow-up would be a visit to a toy museum or a museum of childhood.

Introduction
● Bring in an old toy of your own, along with a photograph of yourself as a child.
● Show the class the toy you have brought in and explain to them that this used to be one of your favourite toys when you were a child.
● Talk to the children about your childhood, your toys and about this special toy that you still have. Talk about who gave it to you. Explain why you were so fond of it and why you still have it.
● Encourage the children to ask questions about the toy and how you played with it as a child.

Main teaching activity
● Organise the children into pairs and ask them to think of one of their own toys which they like most of all.
● They should then make a quick sketch of their toy on a card and write its name.
● Ask them to take turns and talk about their toy or tell a story about it for three or four minutes to their partner.
● Listen to the children as they talk in order to assess their accuracy in using historical terms. For example, I was given this when I was a baby; I used to play with it by myself, but now I share it with my sister, and so on.

Links
● NC English KS1: En1 (1) to speak clearly and with confidence; (2) to listen and respond to others.
● NNS Y1-2: to solve a given problem by sorting, classifying and organising information in simple ways, such as: a simple table, a pictogram or a block graph.
● NC Art and design KS1: (1a) to record from first-hand experience.
● QCA ICT: Unit 1E 'Representing information graphically: pictograms'.

Plenary
● Using the pictures the children have drawn on their small cards, make a simple block graph or pictogram of their favourite toys. Discuss which seem to be the most popular.

Differentiation
Some pairs of children will need prompting in the independent activity to encourage them to talk to their partner and to think of things to say.

Playground games

Objectives
● To find out about the past from first-hand experience of old-fashioned games.

Vocabulary
stretch, jump, hop

Resources
Selection of old-fashioned toys or replicas of toys from the past; a whistle; pictures of children playing with old-fashioned toys (optional).

Background
This lesson makes use of artefacts and old-fashioned games as real playground activities. From using the toys and games they have learned about, the children will begin to understand more clearly what life was like for children in the past and also begin to empathise with them. The use of toys and games in this way is a good introduction for the children to role play and to learning about the past from first-hand experience.

Introduction
● Provide a selection of old-fashioned or replica toys for outdoor use, such as, skipping ropes, marbles, hoops and sticks.
● Talk about and show pictures of children playing these games in the past. Show the children, if necessary, how to use each of the toys. Many toys will be familiar to the children, such as skipping ropes, balls and yo-yos, however, others, such as whips and tops, will need some practice before the children are left to play with them on their own.

Main teaching activity
● Provide time for the children to play these 'old-fashioned' games, possibly during a PE lesson.
● The lesson could begin with some old-fashioned 'drill' exercises.
● Line the children up in straight rows in front of you and demonstrate stretches, up, down and to the sides, with arms and legs, bending movements and balances. Insist on exact imitation of your movements, and that the children all carry out their movements together, just as would have been expected in the past.
● Insist the class stands in perfect lines and allow no talking, turning round, laughing and so on.
● Once the children have practised these movements for a few minutes, give out the toys and observe how the children use them, helping out and advising as necessary.
● Encourage the children to play carefully with the toys if they are expensive replicas.

Plenary
● Invite the children to sit down and talk about their experience. Ask them if they enjoyed the lesson with the old toys. Ask them if they liked the 'drill' and if they would like to do this every day. It would be useful to spend some time comparing the old-fashioned games to the things they play with now.

Links
NC Physical education KS1: (1b) to develop control and coordination in repeating simple actions and skills.

Differentiation
Special consideration will be needed for any children with disabilities during this lesson to enable them to participate as fully as possible. Select appropriate toys. Adult assistance may also be needed.

Making an old-fashioned toy

Objectives
● To find out about the past by making old-fashioned toys.

Vocabulary
paper doll, puppet, hair, eyes, mouth

Resources
Piece of card and a lollipop stick for each child; scraps of material, wool and cotton; crayons or felt-tipped pens; scissors; glue; the photocopiable sheet 'Making an old-fashioned toy' on page 22, one per child and one enlarged copy for display purposes; pictures of old-fashioned dolls.

Links
● NC Design and technology KS1: (2a) to select tools and materials for making a product; (2d) to assemble, join, and combine materials and components; (2e) to use simple finishing techniques.
● QCA Design and technology: Unit 2B 'Puppets'.

Background
Dolls in the Victorian and Edwardian past looked different because they were dressed differently – they often wore hats and had long, curly hair in ringlets. Images from this period in history have been chosen for this activity since they provide a clear contrast with present-day styles, making the activity more understandable for very young children.

Introduction
● Show the class the enlarged version of the photocopiable sheet 'Making an old-fashioned toy' on page 22 and ask the children to guess what it shows.
● Explain that they are going to make their own paper doll puppet and that they can choose which items of clothing, hair and so on that they want to use.
● With the support of other adult helpers, help the children to cut out the basic outline of their paper doll puppet, back it with card and stick it to the lollipop stick, which will act as a handle for the child to hold.

Main teaching activity
● Talk about how to make their paper doll puppet look old-fashioned, using features from the past, which they can choose from their photocopiable sheet. Ask the children how they can tell these features are old-fashioned.
● Again, with adult help as necessary, encourage the children to colour, cut out and stick on whatever they want to add to their doll.
● Explain that they can also draw on other features if they wish, or make curly hair from wool, so that it looks more realistic.

Plenary
● Make a display of the children's paper doll puppets and look at some pictures of old-fashioned dolls.
● The children can use their puppets for role play during the course of the topic.

Differentiation
Many young children find cutting out difficult and will need adult support in this part of the activity. More able children and those in an older age group could be encouraged to create additional items to dress their paper doll.

Poem from the past

Objectives
● To find out about the past from poems.
● To extend vocabulary by using words linked to a topic.

Vocabulary
poem, boat, river

Resources
Enlarged copy of the photocopiable sheet 'Where go the boats?' on page 23; writing materials for each child; selection of key vocabulary from the poem on the board or in a wordbank; home-made boats (optional); computer (optional).

Background
Young children often learn well from poems. This is a teaching and learning strategy that will engage their interest. As well as developing an awareness of the past from the vocabulary they hear, children will also begin to absorb the subject-related language and vocabulary from the past through listening to poems such as those written by Robert Louis Stevenson.

Introduction
● With the whole class look at an enlarged copy of the photocopiable sheet 'Where go the boats?' on page 23.
● Read the poem out loud to the children.

Main teaching activity
● Ask the children why they think the poem is called 'Where Go the Boats?' What is the poem about?
● Look together at the illustrations provided and ask what sort of boats are being described in the poem.
● Talk about the poem as a class. Who is the narrator? Where do they think he or she is?
● Ask the children what the narrator is seeing (rivers, sand and trees, for example) and doing. What sort of toy is the narrator playing with?
● Discuss the different kind of boats in the poem.
● Look at some examples of home-made boats, if you have them available. Ask if anyone has had a toy boat or if anyone has ever made one themselves.
● Use the vocabulary or style of the poem to create a new story or poem about one of the toys in the class collection.
● If possible, carry out the shared writing using a computer, so that the finished version can be printed and displayed with the toy collection.

Plenary
● Encourage the children to tell other poems or stories they have heard or that they make up to the rest of the class. Read some further poems or another story about an old toy.

Differentiation
Less able children could be encouraged to use the computer as an added stimulus to writing and a chance to check spellings. Very able children could be encouraged to write their own verses. Extension activities for the very able, or for those who finish their work quickly, might include making their own paper boat.

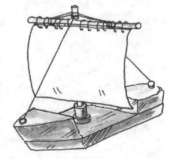

Links
NLS Y1-2 Word level work: vocabulary extension by using words linked to a particular topic.
QCA ICT: Unit 2A 'Writing stories: communicating information using text'.

Pictures of the past

Objectives
● To find out about the past from pictures and photographs.

Vocabulary
photograph, playing, game

Resources
Selection of 19th- or early 20th-century pictures, photographs and illustrations of children playing with toys; enlarged copies of the photocopiable sheet 'Which toys are from long ago?' on page 24, one per child; scissors; glue.

Background
There is a vast range of visual material from Victorian times and later, from which useful teaching resources can be made. As with stories and poems, young children often learn effectively from visual images. These help to bring the past to life and also provide interesting discussion material.

Introduction
● Look at the collection of pictures with the whole class and talk about what is shown in them.
● Ask the children if they can tell what the pictures all have in common or what is special about them (for example, they are all children from the past).
● Talk about how we know they are from the past – ask the children what the various clues are.

Main teaching activity
● Model how to identify the old-fashioned features by asking appropriate questions, such as: *How can we tell these pictures are from the past? What are the clues?*
● Organise the class to work in pairs and give out one or two pictures to each pair.
● Challenge the children to work with their partners to identify more of these old-fashioned features themselves.
● Give each of the children an enlarged copy of the photocopiable sheet 'Which toys are from long ago?' on page 24 and ask them to cut out the pictures of the old-fashioned toys.
● Show them how to stick their cut-out toys in the right places on their illustration of a family scene from the past.
● They can then cut out and stick the whole picture into their book, labelling it 'A Victorian scene'. They could also cut out and stick the modern toys in their book, labelling them 'Modern toys'.

Plenary
● Using the pictures, ask for volunteers to identify the old-fashioned and modern toys. Ask them to explain how they have reached their conclusions. What clues have they spotted?

Links
NLS Y1 T1 Text 14: to write captions; Y1 T2 Text 22-23: to write labels and extended captions.
NC English KS1: En1 (1) to speak clearly and with confidence; (2) to listen and respond to others.

Differentiation
Some younger children will find cutting out and gluing the illustrations difficult and will need extra adult support . The more able writers can add a short sentence, explaining why they have decided a toy is old-fashioned or modern.

Labelling pictures

Objectives
● To communicate their knowledge of history in a variety of ways.

Vocabulary
family, children, father, mother

Resources
Copies of Victorian or Edwardian photographs showing families, some enlarged or on OHT or PowerPoint (copyright permitting), some on paper for the children to use; pencils.

Background
This is an open-ended activity, where each child can reach their own level. Children are required to label as many historical features as they can find on copies of old family photographs. It is helpful to use photographs from a period which is fairly distant in time, since in these the historical features will be more obvious than in more recent pictures and, therefore, easier for the children to find. There is no limit to what can be labelled, and this is a useful activity for assessing children's historical awareness as well as their skills in writing.

Introduction
● Show the class a selection of enlarged family photographs from the past.
● Ask the children if any of them have family photographs at home. How are the old photographs different from their own family's photographs? (They are in black and white; their clothes are different; they are wearing hats, for example.)

Main teaching activity
● Using an enlarged photograph, demonstrate to the whole class how to add labels to the picture.
● Ask the children to suggest features that look old-fashioned, and also words to describe these.
● Show them how to link their words to the pictures with lines or arrows.
● Give either each child, or pairs of children, a copy of an old family photograph and ask them to work independently, or in pairs, to find as many features and to add as many labels as they can.
● Finally, ask the children to write a simple caption for the photograph.

Plenary
● Choose a selection of annotated photographs to show to the class and discuss the labels that have been added, checking for any errors. Are there any features that have been missed?

Differentiation
It may be helpful to pair less able writers with more able children for this activity. Check that the less able partner has the opportunity to contribute ideas and suggestions. More able children, or those who finish quickly, could also be given another picture to work on.

Links
NLS Y1–2 Word level work: vocabulary extension by using words linked to a particular topic; Y1 T1 Text 14: to write captions; Y1 T2 Text 22-23: to write labels and extended captions.

An old-fashioned toyshop

Objectives
- To communicate their knowledge of history in a variety of ways.

Vocabulary
price, ticket, money

Resources
Large table and display board; materials to make a banner for the name of the shop; old-fashioned cash register; old-fashioned apron for the 'shop keeper'; paints and crayons; a collection of old-fashioned toys; labels and price tags for the toys; toy money; shopping bags.

Links
NLS Y1 T1 Text 14: to write captions; Y1 T2 Text 22-23: to write labels and extended captions.
NNS Years 1-2: to recognise coins, find totals, give change and work out which coins to pay.
NC English KS1: En1 (4b) to create and sustain roles.

Background
Through setting up a toyshop, young children not only enjoy first-hand experience and role play, but they also learn more about old-fashioned toys. The link with numeracy is strong in this kind of activity and learning will be enhanced by the connection with out-of-school learning in this shopping activity.

Introduction
- Tell the children that, as a whole class, you are going to turn the play area (or home corner) into a toyshop.
- Explain that the large pieces of furniture, such as a table and display board at the back of the 'shop' area are already in their places, but the name of the shop and the rest of the details need to be completed.
- The first task is to name the shop. Ask the children to suggest what they could call their toyshop. Write their suggestions on the board and decide, by consensus, the name for the shop.

Main teaching activity
- Ask the children what else they need to add or do to make the play area into a toyshop.
- Encourage the children to think about the things that they would expect to find in a shop. Talk about using the shop and what would be needed, such as play money, shopping baskets or bags, labels and price tickets for all the toys.
- Organise the class into small groups. Allocate each group a task, such as painting or colouring in the name for the front of the shop; colouring in the banner which will go over the shop; making the labels and tags; sorting out the money in the cash register; arranging the toys for sale in the 'window'.
- Talk about what might happen when someone visits the toyshop. Ask the class: *What would the shopkeeper say? What would the customers say?*
- The toyshop can then be used by small groups during the topic for the children to act out the role of shopkeeper and customers.

Plenary
- Act out a short role play, with yourself as the shopkeeper and some of the children as shoppers.

Differentiation
Younger and less able children may need support when making labels and price tags. Extend the role-play activity for more able children and encourage them to give 'the correct change' to customers.

A museum timeline of toys

Objectives
● To communicate their knowledge of history in a variety of ways.

Vocabulary
museum, timeline, order, sequence

Resources
Selection of old and new toys from the class collection (see page 7); a table put against a wall for the timeline to be set out on; a simple, blank timeline for the wall behind the display; museum cards: small index cards with headings such as 'object', 'old or new', 'description'; computers (optional).

Links
NLS Y1 T1 Text 14: to write captions; Y1 T2 Text 22-23: to write labels and extended captions; Y2 T3 Text 20: to write non-fiction texts from a given model.
QCA ICT: Unit 1D 'Labelling and classifying'; Unit 2A 'Writing stories: communicating information using text'.

Background
Children find time and chronology one of the most difficult concepts to grasp. It is important, therefore, to provide them with as many varied opportunities to develop this understanding as possible. It is also helpful to begin with 3D objects or pictures and to simply try to get the children to understand how and why they can be put into a sequence. There is no need at this stage in children's learning to concern them with dates and periods, except possibly in passing.

Introduction
● Explain to the children that as a class, you are going to create a museum timeline of toys.
● Choose one of the oldest toys from the class collection and explain to the children that this is going to be one of the toys in the timeline. However, explain that the children will need to write a little bit of information about the toy, just as it is done in real museums.

Main teaching activity
● Draw a large rectangle on the board or overhead projector to represent an information or index card.
● Talk about the features of the toy with the class and compose a few lines to write up on the card, giving the name of the toy, whether it is old or new, and a brief description.

name of object:

age:

material:

description:

● Once the information is complete, take the toy and its card to the timeline area and ask the children: *Where should it go in the timeline?*
● Divide the children into pairs and ask each pair to select a toy from the class collection.
● Give out the 'museum cards' and set the children the task of creating notices for their exhibit, using computers if preferred.
● Ask the children to then create a 'museum timeline' of their toys, placing them in groups or individually in chronological order.
● Finally, the children can make arrows to show their visitors how to follow the route of the timeline.

Plenary
● Discuss how each exhibit has been placed on the timeline, checking for misconceptions and whether they think each toy is in the right place. Visitors, parents and children from other classes can be invited to come and look at the museum timeline.

Differentiation
The museum cards could be differentiated, for example: cards for the less able writers could consist of simple sentences or phrases to complete.

Sorting toys

■ Which toys are old and which are new? Cut them out and put them into two sets for old toys and new toys.

Old toys, new toys

■ Draw lines to match the pictures to the right words. Colour the old toys red and the new toys blue.

plastic aeroplane	
wooden farm animals	
tin soldier	
steam train	
electric train	
car	
plastic blocks	
wooden blocks	

SCHOLASTIC

My old-fashioned toy

■ Draw the toy you have chosen in
the box and then finish the sentences.

My toy is called _____

My toy looks _____

_____

It is coloured _____

I think it is made of _____

It was good to play with long ago because _____

_____

_____

_____

Making an old-fashioned toy

Where go the boats?

Dark brown is the river,
Golden is the sand.
It flows along for ever,
With trees on either hand.

Green leaves a-floating,
Castles of the foam,
Boats of mine a-boating—
Where will all come home?

On goes the river
And out past the mill,
Away down the valley,
Away down the hill.

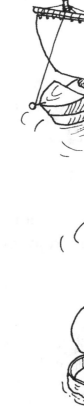

Away down the river,
A hundred miles or more,
Other little children
Shall bring my boats ashore.

Robert Louis Stevenson

Which toys are from long ago?

■ Some of the toys below are new and some are old-fashioned. Which toys would be the right ones for the old-fashioned scene in the above picture?

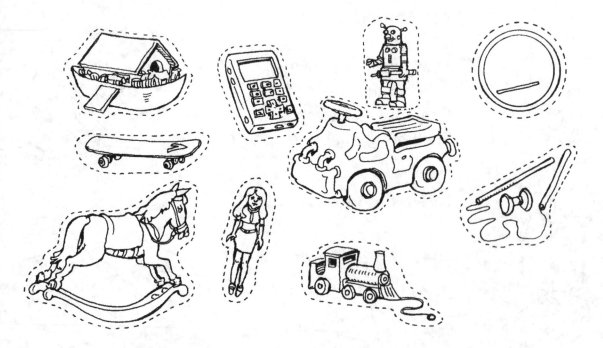

■ Colour and cut out the toys that children would have played with long ago and stick them on the picture.

CHAPTER 2

Homes

The following lesson plans broadly follow the structure for QCA Unit 2 by starting with homes today then looking at homes in the past. A strong focus is placed on exploring familiar activities in the home such as washing clothes and bathtime. Encouraging children to identify similarities and differences between homes now and in the past is a core activity in this unit. Other activities include visits, using artefacts, role play and artwork, which all provide scope for creativity.

	OBJECTIVES	MAIN ACTIVITY
Lesson 1 P	To recognise and talk about different types of homes today, including the children's own. To understand that homes were different in the past.	Children identify types of homes and their features. Then they match labels to pictures of homes and draw their own home.
Lesson 2	To identify differences between homes built at different times. Find out about the past by looking at local houses built at different times. To communicate their knowledge of houses through drawing and writing. To identify features of houses, such as doors and windows.	Children are taken on a field trip to look at different types of homes. They sketch and note their observations.
Lesson 3 P	To place pictures of homes in chronological order. To find out about homes in the past using photographs. To identify differences between homes built at different times.	Sequencing pictures on a timeline, then using the photocopiable sheet, teaches children about chronological order and the differences between old and new houses.
Lesson 4	To find out about the past from historic buildings and artefacts. To identify differences between ways of life at different times.	Children are taken to visit an historic house. They record their observations using sketches and notes.
Lesson 5 P	To find out about home life in the past by looking at and talking about household objects. To ask and answer questions about historical objects. To talk about the main features of household objects and how they might have been used.	In groups, children look at real household items from the past, draw pictures and report on their discoveries to the class.
Lesson 6	To communicate knowledge of household objects in a variety of ways, including ICT. To find out about household objects through observation and research.	After watching a video clip, children create their own pages of an auction sales catalogue, depicting old household items.
Lesson 7	To find out about houses and homes in the past from a range of sources. To design and make models and pictures of houses.	Children research homes both past and present, and make models, paintings or drawings of homes from different periods.
Lesson 8	To find out about home life in the past by listening to an eyewitness account. To ask questions about the past.	An invited visitor talks about their home life in the past. Children ask questions and record answers, both writing and drawing.
Lesson 9 P	To find out about home life in the past, such as washday, using rhymes. To identify differences and similarities between washing today and washing in the past. To give children an awareness of older language and rhyming.	Children ientify and sequence the different stages of washday a long time ago using a rhyme and photographs. They devise appropriate actions to accompany the rhyme.
Lesson 10	To communicate an understanding of home life through play. To find out what rooms were like in the past.	Children create a Victorian kitchen scene, using items that they create together.
Lesson 11 P	To identify similarities and differences between home life now and a long time ago. To make simple observations about keeping clean in the past using pictorial information.	Using pictorial evidence, children consider bathtime in the 1900s and make comparisons to their own experiences. They complete written sentences.
Lesson 12 P	To assess what the children have learned about homes. To reinforce key vocabulary about homes.	Children create a display and prepare a presentation. Key words are revised using a grid and learning is summarised.

What are homes?

Objectives
- To recognise and name different types of homes today.
- To talk about homes including the children's own.
- To understand that homes were different in the past.

Vocabulary
home, house, detached, semi-detached, bungalow, terrace, flat, caravan

Resources
Large pictures or card cut-outs of several different types of home (detached, semi-detached, terrace, bungalow, caravan); word cards to match the pictures; reference books with pictures showing different types of home, but also houses commonly found in historical periods such as Tudor and Victorian; the photocopiable sheet 'What are homes?' on page 38, one per child.

Background
This is a general introduction to the topic, which looks at different types of home. It is clearly important to make links with the children's own homes and to use plenty of visual sources. Differences between homes and houses can be explored.

Introduction
- Show the children a picture of a modern home. Talk about the picture, highlighting words such as 'home', 'house' and 'modern'. What features can the children identify?
- Ask the children whether their own homes look like this. What are the similarities and differences?
- Show the children a picture of an old house, such as a Tudor building. Ask them to look at it carefully and to talk about its main features, such as the wood and the black and white colours. A good example of a Tudor building is Speke Hall near Liverpool (www.national trust.org.uk). Are houses like this still built today?
- Encourage them to discuss the idea that this is an old house. Explain to the children that they are going to find out about different sorts of homes, including modern ones and those built in the past.

Main teaching activity
- Split the class into mixed-ability groups and give each group a set of pictures and word cards.
- Read the word cards with the children and tell them that these are types of homes.
- Ask the children to match the labels to the correct picture and to identify key features of each home.
- Bring the class together and ask each group to talk about one type of home from their set of pictures. Encourage the class to recognise that there are a variety of homes.
- Ask the children what sort of home they live in.
- Give each child to complete the photocopiable sheet 'What are homes?' on page 38.

Plenary
- Conclude the lesson by considering why people live in different types of homes. Bungalows can be of benefit for older people. Caravans are popular with travellers who like to move around.

Links
QCA Design and technology: Unit 1D 'Homes'.
QCA ICT: Unit 1D 'Labelling and classifying'.

Differentiation
Word cards for each room of a home would be useful to support less able children with describing their own homes. More able children could compare pictures of an ordinary house and a very large, luxury home such as Buckingham Palace, highlighting the link between wealth and size of house.

Looking at homes

Objectives
● To identify differences between homes built at different times.
● To find out about the past by looking at local houses built at different times.
● To communicate their knowledge of houses through writing and drawing.
● To identify features of houses, such as doors and windows.

Vocabulary
semi-detached house, detached house, terraced house, new, old, window, door, roof, tiles, slate, brick, stone, glass

Resources
Drawing materials for the children, digital camera (optional).

Links
QCA Design and technology: Unit 1D 'Homes'.
QCA Geography: Unit 1 'Around our school – the local area'.
QCA ICT: Unit 2B 'Creating pictures'.
NC Art and design KS1: (1a) to record from first-hand observation.

Background
Plan a short walk around the local area looking at a variety of houses. Start with modern houses, and, if possible, contrast them with an older house, such as a Victorian terrace. Safety is clearly an issue with this activity and routes must be chosen carefully. Compliance with school and LEA risk assessment policy will be a key component of planning. Fieldwork of this nature requires a high level of adult support, who should be well-briefed beforehand.

Introduction
● Tell the children that you will be taking them on a short walk around the local area to find out about different homes by looking at the outside of them.
● Emphasise the safety aspects of fieldwork, such as obeying instructions when crossing any road and staying on pavements. They all have to stay in their groups and listen to the adult helpers.
● Remind them that it is important that they look at the features of the homes carefully, and that it is also important to record what they see with simple drawings.

Main teaching activity
● Start the walk by looking at modern semi-detached and detached houses. Encourage the children to identify key features, such as doors, windows, walls, chimneys, roofs and garages. Then look at the building materials used, such as bricks, cement, wood, tiles and glass.
● Ask the children to sketch one of these modern homes, showing significant features – these can be labelled later.
● If possible, look at an older house, such as a Victorian terrace. Ask the children to identify differences between the older and modern houses. For example, the older house has no garage; some Victorian and Edwardian houses have sash windows.
● Ask the children to make a drawing of the older house showing clearly any differences they have noticed from the modern houses.

Plenary
● Discuss the key features of modern houses with the children and list similarities and differences they found with the older house.
● For follow-up work, the children can develop and label their drawings of old and new homes. Digital images will allow the children to further develop their observations.

Differentiation
The more able children should be encouraged to make sketches and simple notes. Adult group leaders will need to give support with drawing and, through targeted prompting and questioning, help some children to spot similarities and differences.

Sequencing homes

Objectives
- To place pictures of homes in chronological order.
- To find out about homes in the past using photographs.
- To identify differences between homes built at different times.

Vocabulary
new, old, modern, Victorian, Tudor, chronology

Resources
Enlarged photographs of homes from different historical periods, such as Tudor, Victorian and modern; timeline using string, pegs and date cards for centuries from '1500' to 'The present'; the photocopiable sheet 'Homes: now and then' on page 39; word cards labelled 'Modern', 'Victorian' and 'Tudor' and so on; scissors and glue; paper.

Links
NC English KS1: En1 (1) to speak clearly and with confidence; (2) to listen and respond to others.

Background
Sequencing is a useful introduction to chronological understanding. It is important that children are encouraged to use appropriate vocabulary to describe the homes, such as 'old' and 'new'. An effective but simple timeline can be made with pegs and string. Volunteers can hang up pictures of the houses in the correct order and match the names of periods and dates.

Introduction
- Display the photographs or pictures of a modern brick-built house and a Tudor half-timbered house.
- Talk about the features of the houses, looking at size, shape, building materials and windows.
- Challenge the children to say which is the newest and which is the oldest house, and to give reasons for their decision.

Main teaching activity
- Put up the timeline at the front of the class and peg the two date cards for '1500' on the far left, and 'The present' on the far right.
- Lay out the full selection of pictures of houses at the front of the class and ask for volunteers to place them in chronological order on the timeline using pegs (oldest on the left, newest on the right). Encourage the children to give reasons for their decisions.
- Discuss in simple terms how these houses were built at different times and that names are given to these periods in history. Using the word cards, introduce terms such as 'modern', 'Victorian' and 'Tudor', and add them to the timeline.
- Add the remaining date cards to the timeline to match the appropriate historical period.
- Give each child a copy of the photocopiable sheet 'Homes: now and then' on page 39. Encourage the children to identify various features and to say which is new and which is old.
- Ask the children to cut out the pictures and to sequence them chronologically. The children can then stick the pictures into their books or on paper and add the correct caption and date.
- If there is time, ask the children to write a few similarities and differences between modern and Tudor homes.

Plenary
- Review the timeline and sequencing activities with the children. Ask them why they put the pictures in a particular order.

Differentiation
Some children will need help with cutting out the pictures and labelling. The more able can be challenged by writing full sentences for the section on similarities and differences.

Visiting an historic house

Objectives
● To find out about the past from historic buildings and artefacts.
● To identify differences between ways of life at different times.

Vocabulary
historic, old, new, differences, similarities, guide, tour

Resources
Digital camera or camcorder (obtain permission to photograph or video first); sketching and writing materials for the children; guidance notes for helpers.

Links
QCA Geography: Unit 5 'Where in the world is Barnaby Bear?'
NC English KS1: En1 (4a) to use language and actions to explore and convey situations, characters and emotions.

Background
Organising a visit to an historic house clearly enhances a study of homes. Possible locations include a Victorian stately home or Tudor mansion, but more modest homes should not be overlooked to ensure that the children gain an awareness of how most people lived. The format of visits can vary from a fully guided tour to organised activities, such as role play based on the life of a Victorian kitchen servant. A pre-visit is essential to become familiar with the house, to find out about relevant resources, to prepare a risk assessment and to clarify practical arrangements. A meeting for helpers and written guidance covering their role should be part of the planning process. Children also need to be briefed about the visit.

Introduction
● On arrival at the house, focus the children's attention on the purpose of the visit.
● Discuss the main features of the house that are visible from the outside. How large is the house? What materials it is made from?
● Remind the children of the importance of good behaviour and careful observation to make the most of their visit.

Main teaching activity
● Depending on the organisation, the children can work in small groups with adult helpers, or the whole group can be given a tour.
● There should be plenty of opportunity for them to talk about what they see and to answer questions about the house.
● The children can record their observations by making sketches and brief written comments. Key questions to prompt historical understanding could be: *Is the house new or was it built a long time ago? Would a rich or a poor person have lived in the house?*
● The use of a digital camera or camcorder, if permitted, would clearly be of benefit allowing a good visual record of the visit to be accessed in follow-up sessions. It is best to ask permission during the pre-visit.

Plenary
● Review what the class have found out about the home. Encourage the children to talk about things they have seen. What did they find interesting? What did they find unusual or surprising?
● The effectiveness of an educational visit is strongly influenced by follow-up work, and subsequent lessons need to be carefully linked to what the children experienced.

Differentiation
Some children will need support with their sketching and note making. Adult group leaders have an important role in prompting children to observe key features and to ask questions.

Investigating household objects

Objectives
● To find out about home life in the past by looking at household objects.
● To ask and answer questions about historical objects.
● To talk about the main features of household objects and how they might have been used.

Vocabulary
old, heavy, light, metal, wood, pottery, decorated, object

Resources
Old household objects, such as: oil lamp, flat iron, hot water bottle, butter-pats, carpet beater, pestle and mortar; large photographs showing the objects in their historical settings; the photocopiable sheet 'Exploring a household object' on page 40, one per group.

Links
QCA Science: Unit 1C 'Sorting and using materials'.
NLS Y1 T1 Text 14: to write captions; Y1 T2 Text 22-23: to write labels and extended captions.
NC Design and technology KS1: (4a) Pupils should be taught about the working characteristics of materials.

Background
The use of artefacts allows children to handle genuine historical evidence. Children can discuss what the objects are and what they were used for. Historical skills, such as enquiry and communication, are promoted. It should be relatively easy and cheap to acquire a group of appropriate objects. Appeals to parents are worthwhile, but beware of items of value. Car boot sales and general auction sales are worth considering. Another valuable source is the local museum - its education service will often have artefact collections on popular themes available for hire, usually in the form of replica items.

Introduction
● Show the children an old household object, such as an oil lamp.
● Ask them to carefully observe its different features and to make comments about it, such as its size, weight, shape and colour.
● Prompt them with questions, such as: *What was it used for and where? How does it work?*
● Focus them on historical enquiry by asking the children why they think it is old. Ask them if the object is used today and, if not, what would be used instead.
● Emphasise that historical objects help us to find out what homes were like a long time ago, for example, oil lamps were used because there was no electricity.

Main teaching activity
● Give each group of children a different household object and ask them to investigate and draw it carefully, using the questions on the photocopiable sheet 'Exploring a household object' on page 40.
● Ask each group to tell the rest of the class about their object and what it was used for.
● Move the objects around each group so that the children have an opportunity to handle and investigate the other items. Photographs of the objects in their historical settings could support this activity.

Plenary
● Ask the groups to briefly discuss which of the objects they found the most interesting and why.
● Conclude by using some photographs to reinforce how the objects were used in the home.

Differentiation
Mixed-ability groups should provide mutual support in discussing the objects. Less able children may need help with labelling. The more able could develop their written answers and use reference books.

Auction an old household object

Objectives
● To communicate knowledge of household objects in a variety of ways, including ICT.
● To find out about household objects through observation and research.

Vocabulary
auction, catalogue, antique

Resources
Antique auction catalogue and photocopies of a sample page; OHP; video extract of an auction programme such as *Bargain Hunt* or *Flog It!*; video player; collection of household objects from the past, including decorative as well as utilitarian items; paper and pens or computers.

Links
NLS Y1 T2 Text 23: to write extended captions to describe artefacts; Y2 T3 Text 20: to write non-fiction texts from a given model.
NNS Y1-2: to recognise coins, find totals, give change and work out which coins to pay.
QCA ICT: Unit 1B 'Using a wordbank'.
NC ICT KS1: (5c) talking about the uses of ICT inside and outside school.

Background
In recent years a variety of television programmes like *Flog It!* and *Bargain Hunt* have popularised antique fairs and auctions. Many interesting objects appear from fine ornaments to kitchen utensils. An extension of this lesson could be a visit to the local auction house or a visit to the school by an auctioneer, hopefully with a few artefacts. General house sales will usually have some interesting items of relevance to a topic on homes.

Introduction
● Play a short video clip that shows an interesting household object being auctioned. Ask the children what the object was and how it would be used in a house. Did they know what was happening to the object in the programme? Have they seen programmes like this before on television?
● Discuss with the children how the programme showed the object being sold at an antiques auction and that in the lesson the children will be working on producing their own auction catalogue.

Main teaching activity
● Discuss with the children the words 'antique' and 'auction'.
● Show the children a proper auction catalogue for an antique sale, using an overhead projector to highlight in detail the format of an individual page.
● Ask the children to identify key features on the page, such as a picture, a description of the item and an estimate of value.
● Explain to the children that they are going to produce their own page for an auction catalogue.
● Introduce a range of household objects from the past, including ornaments and items related to housework.
● Children can work in pairs or small groups on one of these objects to produce a picture and a description. This could be done as a large poster format for display purpose and the text could be word-processed. Reference books can help support this activity.

Plenary
● Bring the class together to review progress. Groups can talk about their objects and show the poster. Key vocabulary can be reinforced.

Differentiation
Carefully chosen mixed-ability groupings should allow children to give mutual support. Groups will need close monitoring with the written description. Wordbanks will be helpful.

Modelling houses

Objectives
- To find out about houses and homes in the past from a range of sources.
- To design and make models and pictures of houses.

Vocabulary
modern, Victorian, Tudor

Resources
Pictures of modern, Victorian and Tudor houses; card and paper in various suitable colours; wax crayons; paint; glue; scissors; felt-tipped pens; other craft materials of your choice; reference books; computers (optional).

Links
NC Art and design KS1: (2c) represent observations, ideas, feelings, and design and make images and artefacts. QCA Design and technology: Unit 1D 'Homes'. QCA ICT Unit 2B: 'Creating pictures'.

Background
Key Stage 1 History provides plenty of opportunity for working creatively in art, and this can bring history to life. However, careful organisation is needed, as well as realistic expectations of what children can produce. The starting point for this activity should focus on children finding out about the different types of homes before starting on the creative response. Safety issues when working with equipment, such as scissors, are of course very important.

Introduction
- Show the children some pictures of modern, Victorian and Tudor homes. Ask them to point out key features and ask if they can remember which historical period the houses come from.
- Tell the children that they are going to find out more about these different homes so that they can make models and paintings of them.

Main teaching activity
- Split the class into groups, allocating each a particular house style to investigate.
- Provide each group with appropriate reference books, which the children can use to identify typical features of their house. There is also scope here for use of the internet, with guidance.
- Ask the children to make some sketches of the sort of house they are going to model and to highlight important features.
- Possibilities for creative work include:
  - making simple models of houses using cardboard boxes (features of the house, such as doors and windows, can be produced on separate coloured pieces of paper and glued on)
  - drawing the outline of a Tudor house, for example, on cream paper, cutting up strips of white paper and colouring them brown using crayon and gluing the strips onto the house shape to represent the wooden timber framing (a piece of straw-coloured sugar paper could be added for the roof and doors and windows could be similarly made)
  - using drawing and painting to portray houses from different historical periods (charcoal drawings or using an ICT graphics package are interesting alternatives to painting).

Plenary
- Bring the class together and review the progress made. Ask each group to present their model or picture and use this as a resource for explaining what they have found out about their period house.

Differentiation
All groups will need very close support and the use of adult helpers would be of considerable value.

Oral history: home life

Objectives
● To find out about home life in the past by listening to an eyewitness account.
● To ask questions about the past.

Vocabulary
oral history, visitor, guest, interview, housework, leisure

Resources
Artefacts; photographs of home life; reference books and Big Books; interview sheet with key questions, one copy per child.

Background
Oral history has made a very significant contribution to academic history in recent years and also has much to offer to class work. Careful preparation for this activity ensures an appropriate choice of visitor who is aware of the nature of the session and their contribution to it. It should be possible to find someone who can talk with confidence about home life in the 1940s or 1950s, when they were a child. Links might also be possible with an old people's home. Visitors should be encouraged to bring in any artefacts or photographs which can form the focus of discussion. Reference books, such as Big Books, might be a useful resource for the visitor.

Introduction
● Ask the children how we can find out about home life in the past.
● Write key words on the board, such as reference books, photographs and artefacts.
● Encourage the children to identify the value of talking with older people like their parents and grandparents about the past.
● Explain that a visitor is coming in to talk about home life in the past. With the children, draw up a list of questions which they could ask the visitor about homes.

Main teaching activity
● Introduce the visitor to the class. The format of the session might vary according to the wishes of the visitor but could consist of an initial short talk followed by questions.
● Allowing the visitor to talk about photographs or old artefacts they have brought in from their home can make the session come alive for the children.
● Questions asked by you and the children could help to structure the session. For example: *Where did you live? What sort of house did you live in? What did it look like on the outside and inside? What rooms did it have? What do you remember about housework and leisure time?*
● Give a copy of the interview sheet to the children and encourage them to record some key points using simple text and drawings.

Plenary
● Review the progress the children have made on the interview sheet, which reinforces what they found out about home life in the past. Children can ask the visitor any final questions. Briefly introduce the term 'oral history' and discuss its meaning.

Differentiation
Terminology used by the visitor needs careful monitoring to ensure that the children understand what is being related to them. Less able children will need help with writing their answers.

Links
Non-statutory guidelines: PSHE and citizenship KS1: (5e) meet and talk with people, for example, with outside visitors.
NC English KS1: En1 (1) to speak clearly and with confidence; (2) to listen and respond to others.

▉ 33

A washday rhyme

Objectives
● To find out about home life in the past, such as washday, using rhymes.
● To identify differences and similarities between washing today and washing in the past.
● To give children an awareness of older language and rhyming.

Vocabulary
washday, dolly peg, dolly tub, mangle, scrubbing brush, soap, washboard, squeeze, rhyme

Resources
Enlarged copy of the poem 'Washday at Home'; enlarged pictures of different washday activities; the photocopiable sheet 'Washday in the 1900s' on page 41, one per child; reference books (optional); glue and scissors.

Links
NLS Y1 T2 Text 11: to learn and recite action poems and rhymes.

Background
Nursery rhymes and action verses, such as 'Pease Porridge Hot' and 'Here We Go Round the Mulberry Bush', are a valuable source for introducing children to life in the past. This lesson uses 'Washday at Home'. As well as their historical value, these verses are useful for early language development and introducing new vocabulary.

Introduction
● Read the rhyme 'Washday at Home' with the children.

> Mother's washing, Mother's washing,
> Rub, rub, rub.
> Picked up Johnny's little shirt
> And threw it in the tub.
>
> Mother's washing, Mother's washing,
> Scrub, scrub, scrub.
> Picked up Mary's little frock
> And threw it in the tub.
>
> Mother's washing, Mother's washing,
> Wring, wring, wring.
> Picked up Tommy's little coat
> And hung it on some string.
>
> Mother's finished, Mother's finished,
> Hip hooray!
> Now we'll have our clothes all clean
> To wear for school today.

● Ask the children what sort of writing it is. Introduce the word 'rhyme' and discuss what it means.
● Focus carefully on the words. What is happening in the rhyme? Highlight key words like *tub*, *rub*, *scrub*, *wring* and *hung*.
● Emphasise that the washing is being done by hand.
● Ask the children how washing is done in their own homes.

Main teaching activity
● Read the first verse again. Using pictures, discuss the different stages of the washday process: filling the dolly tub with hot water; adding soap and then the dirty clothes; using the dolly peg to churn the clothes in the water; using a washboard to clean the clothes; scrubbing with a brush and soap; squeezing water out of the clothes using a mangle; hanging out the washing to dry.
● Give each child a copy of photocopiable sheet page 41, 'Washday in the 1900s' and ask them to complete and order the sentences.
● Encourage the children in groups to think of actions that could go with the words in 'Washday at Home'.

Plenary
● Ask the children to sequence pictures of washday activities correctly as a class and to talk about what each picture shows.
● Read the rhyme again and add the actions to go with the words.

Differentiation
Less able children might need help with the sentence completion activity and setting out the pictures in their books. More able children could use reference books to find out more about washday.

A room from long ago

Objectives
● To communicate an understanding of home life through play.
● To find out what rooms were like in the past.

Vocabulary
range, oven, coal, kettle, sink, pots, fender

Resources
Range of relevant artefacts and costumes; mannequin for dressing as a Victorian servant; pictures or a short video clip of Victorian kitchens and kitchen servants at work; flipchart and pen.

Links
QCA Design and technology: 1D 'Homes'. NC Art and design KS1: (2b) to try out tools and techniques and apply these to materials and processes, including drawing; (2c) to design and make images and artefacts. NC English KSI: En1 (4b) to create and sustain roles individually and when working with others.

Background
Children's understanding of homes from a long time ago can be facilitated by re-creating a room scene in a corner of the classroom. There are several possibilities for this, such as a living room, kitchen, laundry or bathroom from, for example, the Victorian period. This activity requires much careful planning and preparation, and takes the example of a Victorian kitchen. An appeal to parents should yield some items, but be careful about accepting responsibility for valuable or fragile objects. Household clearance and car boot sales can yield a surprisingly cheap range of items. Another option is to hire artefact collections from the local museum education service.

Introduction
● Discuss with the children how to transform a classroom corner into a room from a long time ago, such as a Victorian kitchen.
● Show the children a few large photographs of a Victorian kitchen or a short video clip.
● Ask the children to identify the main features and objects in a Victorian kitchen scene.
● List these on flipchart paper and sketch out a possible plan to include items, such as a range or fireplace, table, sink, shelving and a window.

Main teaching activity
● Divide the children into groups. Discuss the tasks that need to be done in order to create their room from a long time ago.
● Activities might include:
  ● writing captions for the artefacts which have been assembled
  ● making some kitchen objects out of cardboard, such as butter-pats and rolling-pins
  ● putting the artefacts in the correct area
  ● making parts of the main scenery, such as the range (a cardboard cut-out), with adult help.
● Children could create pictures of scenes and appropriate objects, if the artefacts are not available, for inclusion within the display.
● When the scene is completed, small groups can engage in role play, preferably using costumes.

Plenary
● Give the children opportunities to use the kitchen scene actively and encourage them to talk about what life was like in the past.

Differentiation
Groups will need careful organisation, particularly when making items for the scene, and adult helpers would be invaluable. Mixed-ability groups will be useful for preparing the role play.

Bathtime: now and then

Objectives
● To identify similarities and differences between home life now and a long time ago.
● To make simple observations about keeping clean in the past using pictorial information.

Vocabulary
soap, flannel, tin bath, shower, brush

Resources
Modern bathroom items (such as soap, flannel, bubble bath, shower gel and bath brush); enlarged picture of bathtime in the 1900s; a tin bath (optional); the photocopiable sheet 'Bathtime: now and then' on page 42, one per child.

Links
NC Art and design KS1: (1a) to record from first-hand observation, experience and imagination.

Background
Bathtime is an interesting subject within a topic on homes, allowing comparisons to be made between now and the Victorian period. Only from the 1900s did bathrooms become commonplace in the homes of ordinary people. Before this, baths were usually taken in the kitchen or public bathhouses, which were a popular alternative in towns. Another dimension worth looking at is the home life of the wealthy, as they had bathrooms well before the majority of people.

Introduction
● Show the children some bathroom items.
● Ask them what these items are used for, encouraging the children to make links to personal washing, bathtime and keeping clean.
● Discuss the key features of modern bathrooms, such as a bath, shower and hot water. What are the children's own bathrooms like?
● Tell the children that keeping clean is important and that they will be comparing bathrooms today with bathtime a long time ago.

Main teaching activity
● Using an enlarged picture, show the children a typical bathtime scene from the early 20th century. If available, show them a tin bath to emphasise the contrast between bathtime now and in the past.
● Ask them to identify differences with bathtime today, such as the lack of a proper bathroom and the use instead of a portable tin bath that needed filling by hand.
● Encourage the children to think of reasons for these differences, for example: the lack of running water, houses were not built with bathrooms and so on.
● Give each child a copy of the photocopiable sheet 'Bathtime: now and then' on page 42, showing the bathtime scene in the kitchen.
● Ask the children to identify what is the same and what is different, compared with their own bathtime, and to record their conclusions using drawings and brief text.

Plenary
● Ask the children to say what similarities and differences they identified and to read out their completed sentences. Encourage the children to think about what it must have been like bathing under such difficult conditions. Emphasise that fetching and heating the water took a lot of effort. Many people did not bath even once a week.

Differentiation
The less able might need help listing some similarities and differences. More able children could be given extension work, such as making inferences from a picture of a proper bathroom in a wealthy person's house.

What have we learned about homes?

Objectives
● To assess what the children have learned about homes.
● To reinforce key vocabulary about homes.

Vocabulary
old, new, past, modern

Resources
Items that relate to the topic of homes in the past; word cards; the photocopiable sheet 'Homes word grid' on page 43, one per child.

Background
It is important with any unit of work to allow children to reflect upon and to show what they have learned. This lesson allows them, in a limited way, to demonstrate learning both orally and in writing, as well as engaging in simple self-assessment. For the teacher, it provides an opportunity for assessment although it must be stressed that this should be a continuing theme through all lessons.

Introduction
● Invite the children to create a display of the items you have collected, relating to homes. This will include the children's paintings and models, the artefacts and photographs, and the display scene.
● Tell the children they will be thinking about what they have learned about homes over the past lessons.
● Using word cards, revise key vocabulary about homes by asking the children to explain the meanings.

Main teaching activity
● Focus on the display items produced by the children and draw their attention to particular objects of interest, relating them to what they have learned previously.
● Tell the children that they are going to work in groups to briefly talk about a particular display item and what it tells us about homes.
● Allocate an item or part of a display scene to each group and give them some preparation time for them to decide what they can say.
● Discuss with each group what they might want to say about homes and emphasise that all group members must contribute.
● Before they give their brief talk, give each child a copy of the photocopiable sheet 'Homes word grid' on page 43. Ask the children to complete the word grid and to summarise what they have learned about homes.

Plenary
● Bring the class together. Work through the photocopiable sheet, asking for volunteers to give their answers.
● Finally, let each group go to the display area and talk about their allocated display item. You may wish to ask simple questions to prompt the children, if necessary.

Links
NC English KS1: En1 (1) to speak clearly and with confidence; (2) to listen and respond to others.

Differentiation
Mixed-ability groups should facilitate effective presentations. The more able children should be encouraged to write extended sentences. Less able children will need help with listing some key points about what they have learned.

What are homes?

Here are some pictures of houses. Draw a line to match the words in the wordbank to the correct picture.

detached house   caravan   terraced house   bungalow

Draw a picture of your own home and make a list of some of the rooms.

1 _____

2 _____

3 _____

4 _____

5 _____

6 _____

Homes: now and then

◾ These homes were built at different times. Cut them out and put them in order, with the oldest first and the newest last.

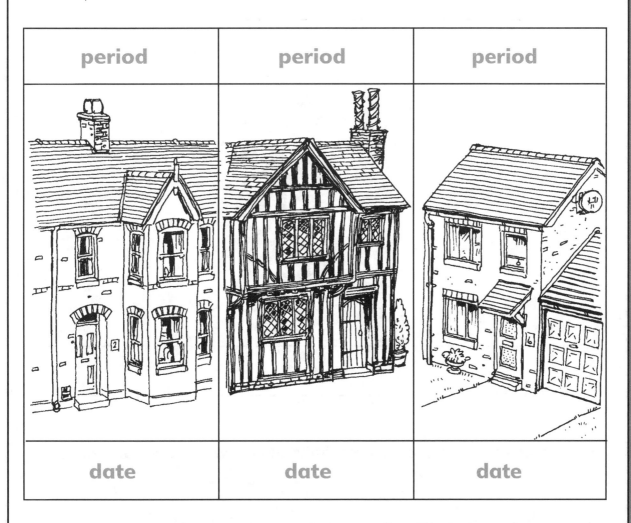

period	period	period
date	date	date

◾ Next, cut out the labels and dates. Match them with the correct picture. When you have got them right, stick them in your book.

1500

◾ Look at the modern home and the Tudor home. On a separate sheet of paper, or in your book, write down what things are the same and what things are different.

Exploring a household object

Look very carefully at your object and make a drawing of it in the box below. Add some labels to show different parts.

My object is a _____

Look again at the object very carefully and answer these questions.

What colour is it? _____

Is it heavy or light? _____

What is it made from? _____

Is there any writing on it? _____

What would it have been used for? _____

Who would have used it? _____

Washday in the 1900s

◼ Colour in these pictures showing washday a long time ago.

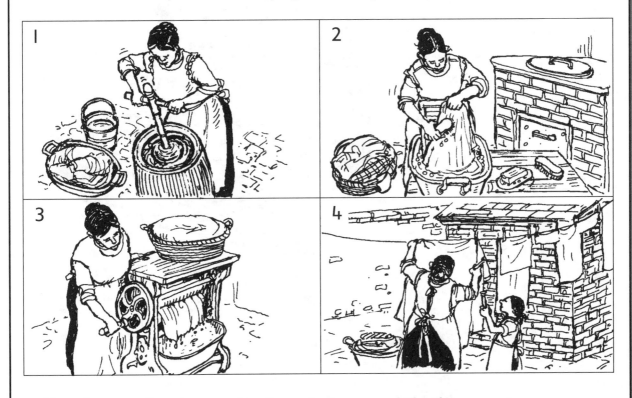

◼ Use the wordbank to write the missing words in these sentences.
◼ The sentences are in the wrong order. Match the sentences with the correct pictures and write the numbers in the boxes.

☐ Some dirty clothes were cleaned by using a scrubbing brush,

_____ and a _____.

☐ The washing was hung on the _____ _____ to _____.

☐ Dirty clothes were washed in a _____ _____ using a _____ _____.

☐ A _____ was used to _____ the water out of the washing.

> dolly tub   washing line   soap   dolly peg
>
> mangle   washboard   dry   squeeze

Bathtime: now and then

This picture shows what bathtime was like a long time ago. Now think about your own bathtime.

What is the same?	What is different?
•	•
•	•
•	•

■ On the back of this sheet, draw or write about something that we do not use anymore and something that has not changed.

■ Use the wordbank to complete these sentences.

The house in the picture did not have a _____. On bath night

a _____ _____ was put in the _____ in front of the fire.

Water was _____ and then carried to the bath.

| heated | tin bath | bathroom | kitchen |

Homes word grid

Use these clues to fill in the word grid.

1 Windows are made of this material.

2 These homes are all joined together in a row.

3 This home can move!

4 Used on washday to squeeze water out of clothes.

5 The name given to a home built a long time ago, often with a wooden frame.

6 Found on the roof of a house and lets out smoke.

7 Used in a Victorian kitchen for heating and cooking.

1	G						
2	T						
3	C						
4	M						
5	T						
6	C						
7	R						

What have you learned about homes?

What have you enjoyed about this topic?

CHAPTER 3

Castles

This chapter is based on QCA Adapted Unit 'What were castles like a long time ago?'. The lessons build on work on 'Homes'. It is important for children to begin the topic by investigating what is familiar to them, namely their own home. From this starting point, they can begin to see the significance of castles as a type of home in the past and to relate to the study of them in a meaningful way.

Children should begin to understand the distinctions between a home today and a castle, as well as to think about similarities. They will learn how castles have changed over time, from largely being defensive structures in Norman times to developing into more domestic residences in the Tudor era. In more recent examples of castles used as homes in the 19th and early 20th centuries, kitchen gardens and formal gardens were created to serve domestic needs.

	OBJECTIVES	MAIN ACTIVITY
Lesson 1	To understand that people live in different types of homes. To recognise common external features of homes. To record observations appropriately.	Children look at different types of homes during a walk in the local area. They make comparisons and sketch or photograph examples.
Lesson 2	To identify the key features of the inside of a home.	Focusing on rooms of their choice, children draw and label detailed pictures and create a display.
Lesson 3 P	To identify and compare key features found in homes today and in castles. To give reasons for some of the features that they have identified in castles.	As a whole class, children look at cross-sections of a house and a castle and list features of both. In groups, they consider similarities and differences.
Lesson 4	To find out about the past from historic buildings. To identify key features to be found in castles. To ask and answer questions about the past.	Children visit a castle and make observations through discussion, note-taking, sketching and labelling.
Lesson 5	To find out about the past from historic buildings. To begin to understand that the past is represented in different ways.	Children find out which features of castles were meant for defence. They read word cards and draw and label their own pictures.
Lesson 6	To communicate their learning about castles through role play. To apply their knowledge and understanding of life in a castle a long time ago.	A Great Hall is created and children role play life in a castle in the past, taking the parts of lords, ladies, servants, cooks and soldiers.
Lesson 7 P	To find out about the past from written sources. To apply their knowledge and understanding of life in a castle a long time ago.	Children learn about food eaten in castles in the past. They look at an example of a medieval menu and then create a menu for the role-play area.
Lesson 8	To find out about the past from written sources. To apply their knowledge and understanding of life in a castle a long time ago.	Following a recipe and illustration, children make Tudor gingerbread.
Lesson 9 P	To learn about people who used to live in castles. To learn about different ways of life in the past. To learn the vocabulary of chronology.	Children listen to a story about the work of a medieval cook, then, in shared writing, they create their own tale about someone who works in a castle.
Lesson 10 P	To find out about the past from stories.	Children listen to a story about hunting in the past and then create a sequence of pictures and sentences retelling the story.
Lesson 11	To find out about the past from pictures and symbols.	The meanings of heraldic symbols are explored, leading children to produce their own coat of arms.
Lesson 12 P	To place pictures of castles in chronological sequence.	Children sequence pictures of castles, identifying the features that show whether they are older or newer.

What sorts of homes do people live in today?

Objectives
● To understand that people live in different types of homes.
● To recognise common external features of homes.
● To record observations appropriately.

Vocabulary
bungalow, terraced house, detached house, semi-detached house, flat

Resources
Packs of pictures showing different types of homes; cameras; sketching materials.

Links
NLS Y1-2 Word level work: vocabulary extension by using words linked to a particular topic.
NC Art and design KS1: (1a) to record from first-hand observation.
QCA Geography: Unit 1 'Around our school - the local area'.

Background
Plan a short walk to look at houses in the local area, ensuring that parental permission is obtained and that adequate adult supervision is available. Complete a risk assessment, especially if the walk involves negotiating busy roads. There is a great diversity of homes that people live in today. Children will need to have thought about this and also to have made observations, so that they can use this experience as a basis for comparing homes in the past. This lesson could take up one or two sessions, with the children doing the follow-up artwork on another day rather than immediately after the walk.

Introduction
● Introduce the children to the idea that people live in different types of homes by showing them a variety of pictures. Include pictures of bungalows, flats, caravans, terraced and detached houses.
● Discuss with the children the differences between the homes, for example: some are small or large; some have many rooms, while others only have a few. Talk about the names of the different homes.

Main teaching activity
● Take the class on a short walk to look at homes in the local area.
● Discuss the similarities and differences between the different homes they see.
● Ask why and how the homes look different.
● Ask the children what is the same about all of the homes. Make a note of their answers.
● Encourage them to observe details, such as building materials, styles and number of windows and doors.
● With adult support, encourage the children to draw or photograph the homes and details they observe.

Plenary
● Back in school, review the key features of the homes the children have seen and make a list of their names.
● Explain that in the past, some people lived in large homes called castles and that many of the things they have noticed about the homes they have seen today would have been found in castles, which they will soon be learning about.

Differentiation
Younger or less able children will need support in adding detail to their sketches and in writing labels or captions for their pictures. Encourage more able children to write full sentences under their illustrations, giving details of what they observed.

Inside a home

Objectives
- To identify the key features of the inside of a home.

Vocabulary
door, window, hall, kitchen, dining room, living room, bedroom, toilet

Resources
Collection of pictures showing different home interiors and rooms; drawing and colouring materials; paper; list of key vocabulary on the board or in a wordbank.

Background
The day before this lesson, give the children some sketching paper and ask them to choose one room in their own home to draw. Remind them that they will need their picture the next day. As in Lesson 1, children will need to have thought about what homes are like inside and also to have made observations, so that they can use this experience as a basis for comparing to homes in the past.

Introduction
- Discuss what a home is with the class. Prompt the children with questions such as, *What do we need inside our home? What do we have in a home that we do not have in a school? What makes a home? What is a home?*
- Look at the collection of pictures that show different home interiors and rooms. Ask the children to group them together and to tell you what each room is called, writing the types of room as headings on the board.
- Ask the children to identify common features in these rooms and list their words under the headings.

Main teaching activity
- Ask the children to use their sketches made at home to make a larger, more detailed picture of the inside of their home.
- Suggest that they can draw one or more rooms, such as their bedroom or the kitchen. They can choose from the key words on the board to label their pictures.
- Give the children time to finish their work. Then invite the children to sort the pictures into groups. You could suggest that all pictures of the same rooms are grouped together, or that the children attempt to make 'complete houses' using different rooms in one set.
- Let the children work together to make a display of their pictures, using the grouping you have decided on. Encourage them to add captions and written explanations to the display.

Plenary
- Talk about the details the children have included in their pictures and compare them to the range of different home interiors in the pictures that you collected.
- Ask the children what things are the same about all these pictures. Talk about what we need in particular rooms. Conclude by saying that in the next lesson they will be looking at a castle, to see what kind of home this is.

Differentiation
The more able children might be able to draw a cross-section of their home. Less able children will need support in labelling their pictures.

Links
NLS Years 1–2 Word level work: vocabulary extension by using words linked to a particular topic.
NC Art and design KS1: (1a) to record from first-hand observation; (2c) to design and make images.

Comparing homes and castles

Objectives
- To identify and compare key features found in homes today and in castles.
- To give reasons for some of the features that they have identified in castles.

Vocabulary
live, eat, sleep, fight, defend

Resources
Whiteboard and markers; writing materials; the photocopiable sheet 'Cross-section of a home' on page 57 and the photocopiable sheet 'Cross-section of a castle keep' on page 58, both enlarged for display; pictures of different types of castles.

Links
NLS Y1–2 Word level work: vocabulary extension by using words linked to a particular topic.
NC English KS1: En1 (3) to join in a discussion as members of a group.

Background
At different times in the past, castles were built to defend a settlement or population and they also functioned as homes for their owners, who were generally monarchs and their nobles. Castles had many similar features to the homes of more ordinary people, though they were, of course, much larger. In times of danger, the population of a town or city would gather inside the castle walls for protection against invaders.

Introduction
- Discuss what children think of as home. Briefly review the types of home they have learned about.
- Ask them about other types of homes they have heard of, and introduce the idea of a castle being a home.
- Look at pictures of different types of castles, discussing their features and thinking about who might have lived in them.

Main teaching activity
- Display the enlarged photocopiable sheet showing a cross-section of a home. Discuss with the children what each room is used for.
- Working with the whole class, create a list of the key features of the home shown on the sheet, such as front door, window, roof, living room, bedroom, bathroom.
- Next use the photocopiable sheet showing a cross-section of a castle to identify the purpose of the different parts of the castle.
- Organise the class into small groups, making sure they can all see the two lists of key features. Ask the groups to discuss what is different in the two lists and what is the same. The more able children should act as note-takers and write down what their group thinks, in order to create lists of the similarities and differences. Can the children think of any reasons for the features of a castle?

Plenary
- Gather the groups together and ask them to report back to the whole class on their discussions and compare their findings.
- Tell the class about the key differences in the functions of a home and a castle. Long ago, people built castles to defend themselves from attackers, but they also used to live in castles as their homes.

Differentiation
Some children will need support in reading the lists and remembering the discussions about homes and castles. More able children will be able to make their own notes of the differences. Mixed-ability groups might be helpful in supporting the less able readers and writers.

Visit to a castle

Objectives
- To find out about the past from historic buildings.
- To identify key features to be found in castles.
- To ask and answer questions about the past.

Vocabulary
walls, moat, battlements, portcullis

Resources
Notes for helpers; sketching and writing materials; brochures and postcards of the castle (some organisations provide resource packs, for example, some castles run by English Heritage).

Background
It is vital to prepare in advance for the visit, gaining consent from parents and carers to take the children on the trip first. Arrange a pre-visit to identify key teaching points and suitable resources and facilities, such as toilets, lunch facilities and potential working areas. Prepare a risk assessment for the site. Many organisations welcome educational visits and will arrange a guided tour. In school, organise a team of helpers and meet with them to discuss your objectives, the day's main activities and their role. If possible, collect published resources to help your class prepare for the visit. Photographs are a helpful resource, but you must get permission to use them first. The Historic Houses Association (www.hha.org.uk) and English Heritage (www.english-heritage.org.uk) provide information about local castles.

Introduction
- Gather the children outside the castle and encourage them to look at the main features of the castle's exterior.
- Prompt the children with questions such as: *Why was the castle built here? What features would help the people who lived there?*
- Remind the children about the importance of good behaviour and staying in their groups.

Main teaching activity
- Ask the children to think about who lived in the castle. Ask them to consider where the people lived inside and whether it was their home. What do the children think it would have been like living in a castle? Challenge the children to think about these questions during their visit and to see how many they can answer at the end of the day.
- Divide the class into small groups, led by the helpers, and encourage the children to make observations, notes and drawings, and to discuss the castle.
- During the visit, keep circulating around the groups to ensure that the children are working well and gaining from the experience.
- Encourage the children to sketch what they see (such as rooms, artefacts and castle features) for use after the visit.

Plenary
- Briefly discuss what the children have noticed and any answers they may have found to the questions posed at the beginning of the day. Collect the children's artwork and notes for use back in school.

Links
NC Geography KS1: (1a) to ask geographical questions; (2a) to use geographical vocabulary.

Differentiation
The most able children will be able to make notes and write extended sentences about the key places they visit in the castle. Younger or less able children will need adult support in making notes and sketches and in identifying key features.

Using photographs of a castle

Background
Castles were built on a grand scale, on the whole, so that many people could shelter in them from attackers, and so that they could hold soldiers to defend them. The windows in early castles were made deliberately narrow for protection, but they also allowed archers to fire arrows at attackers outside the walls. The walls were also thick for defensive reasons, in the same way that castles were usually built on a hill or high ground, and surrounded by water - all further attempts to make them harder to break into by attackers.

This lesson focuses on the defensive features of a castle and there is also an opportunity to look at the castle's living quarters.

Introduction
● Display pictures of the castle at the front of the class or give a set of pictures to each group of children. Ask the children to use these pictures to think about how a castle is built to defend a town.
● Prompt the children with questions such as: *Why were castles so big? Why are the windows small and narrow? Why are the walls so thick? Why do some castles have moats?*
● Ask the children if they can think of any other features of the castle that might be used for defence purposes, such as the portcullis, keep and battlements.

Main teaching activity
● Give the children the sets of word cards containing the key features of the castle you have covered with the children.
● Working in pairs or small groups, invite the children to match the words to the pictures that are on display or that you have given to the children. Ask for volunteers to read the words out to the class.
● Provide materials for the children to draw their own castles and then label their drawings with the word cards.

Plenary
● On a large wall, display your poster or enlarged picture of the castle. Ask the children to place the large word cards in the correct position, labelling the key defensive features of the castle.

Differentiation
It will be helpful to organise the children to work in mixed-ability groups for the initial labelling activity, so that the better readers can help the less able match the word cards to the pictures. Encourage more able children to write their own labels, rather than gluing the word cards on to their pictures.

Creating a Great Hall

Objectives
● To communicate their learning about castles through role-play.
● To apply their knowledge and understanding of life in a castle a long time ago.

Vocabulary
lords, ladies, servants, entrance, Great Hall

Resources
Picture of a Great Hall; cardboard castle wall with battlements and a cut-out archway for an entrance; craft materials (including paints, felt-tipped pens, crayons, paper, scissors and glue); benches inside the walls to allow 'soldiers' to get up and see over the battlements; suitable items for role play, such as: dressing-up clothes, tables, chairs, tablecloth, items for mealtimes (for example, trenchers, blunt knives, and goblets).

Background
This activity allows children to strengthen their understanding of what life was like in a castle in the past by acting out their ideas. You may wish to divide this lesson into several sessions, depending on the level of detail you decide on for the role-play area. Many familiar household tasks, such as cooking, washing and cleaning, would have been carried out in a castle. Other tasks included entertaining important noble guests and defending the castle. The Great Hall would have been used for banquets and entertaining important guests. It was the focal point of the castle and was often the most elaborately furnished, with tapestries and heavy wooden furniture.

Introduction
● Display a picture of a Great Hall and tell the children that they will be making a 'front wall' with battlements and, within these walls, a small version of a 'Great Hall'.
● Set up the wall and paint outlines of the stones in the wall. Add pictures, in the style of tapestries, and flags on the battlements. Make any other items you require, for example, shields for the soldiers.
● Arrange tables to form a long banqueting table and put chairs on one side of the table only ('servants' could then serve the food more easily). A chair can be placed at the head of the table for the 'lord' or 'lady'. Cover the table with a long cloth.

Main teaching activity
● Discuss the roles of the lord and lady of a castle with the children.
● Talk about special events that might have happened, such as grand processions when important visitors arrived, banquets and feasts. Discuss the roles of different people when there were visitors, such as the cooks and servants, and the soldiers who looked out for attackers while standing at the battlements.
● Organise the children into small groups and provide each group with a variety of objects, such as dressing-up clothes, cups and plates.
● While the rest of the class is occupied with other activities, allow one group at a time to re-enact life in the Great Hall, taking the roles of lords, ladies, servants, cooks, and soldiers.

Plenary
● Once each group has taken their turn in the Great Hall, discuss what other rooms could be created inside the castle. Make plans to change the role-play area into a different room, such as the kitchen, each subsequent week of the topic and to make further artefacts .

Differentiation
Mixed-ability groups will be useful in these activities, so that the less able children can be prompted with ideas and talk by the more able.

Links
NLS Y1-2 Word level work: vocabulary extension by using words linked to a particular topic.
NC English KS1: En1 (4) to participate in a range of drama activities, such as role play.

Menu for a meal

Objectives
● To find out about the past from written sources.
● To apply their knowledge and understanding of life in a castle a long time ago.

Vocabulary
menu, meal, banquet, feast, guests

Resources
Different examples of menus; the photocopiable sheet 'Menu for a meal in a castle' on page 59, enlarged for display; books containing accounts and illustrations of meals in the past; pictures of medieval foods (optional); pens and paper.

Links
NLS Y2 T1 Text 16: to use models from reading to organise instructions sequentially.

Background
The menu on the photocopiable sheet on page 59 is an example of an ordinary everyday meal at the lord's table in a castle. A banquet would be several times larger than the amount shown here, with sweet dishes served at intervals between the meat and fish courses. When visitors came to the castle, especially if it was the monarch, large banquets were laid on to impress the guests. Many foods were eaten which are no longer common, such as whole roast pig or boar, suckling pig, swan or peacock. Some of these animals would be kept in the castle grounds, while others would be taken from the town or caught on hunting expeditions. Large banquets had many courses in comparison to today with very elaborate, colourful 'sweetmeats' to end the meal.

Introduction
● Display your examples of menus and discuss them with the class. Prompt the children with questions such as: *What sort of writing is this? Why is it arranged like a list? What sort of information does it contain?*
● Look with the whole class at some illustrated books about meals in the past. Discuss the kinds of foods that were eaten, such as goose, swan or suckling pig.

Main teaching activity
● Together, look at the example of a menu for a lord's meal provided on the photocopiable sheet 'Menu for a meal in a castle' on page 59. Talk about the different foods and give explanations for any that the children's have not heard of before.
● Discuss with the children how the menu is arranged.
● Ask the children to work in pairs to decide and write down what they would like on a menu for a meal in a castle. Invite volunteers to share their menus with the rest of the class.
● During a shared writing session, compile a menu from the children's ideas and ask the children to illustrate it.
● Show the children how to fold the menu so that it can stand on the lord's table.
● Encourage the children to use the menu in the role-play area.

Plenary
● Compare the kinds of food that would have been eaten in the past with the things that the children put on their own menu.

Differentiation
Encourage less able children to come up with one or two ideas for a menu. More able readers and children from an older age group will be able to use information books to develop their ideas.

Food for a banquet

Objectives
● To find out about the past from written sources.
● To apply their knowledge and understanding of life in a castle a long time ago.

Vocabulary
cooking, ginger, gingerbread, colour, mixing

Resources
Recipe ingredients; mixing bowls and spoons; knife for cutting (teacher use); a 'charger', or large plate, to serve the gingerbread on; an enlarged copy of the recipe and illustration on this page; modern gingerbread.

Background
Gingerbread was originally made from breadcrumbs mixed with honey and spices. Extra adult support may be needed when mixing the gingerbread to ensure adequate standards of hygiene. Check with parents and carers if the children have any allergies or dietary requirements before the lesson.

Tudor gingerbread
Ingredients
500g clear honey
500g fresh white breadcrumbs
2 teaspoons ground cinnamon
2 teaspoons ground ginger
1 teaspoon ground black pepper
Red food colouring
Whole cloves to decorate

1 Mix the ingredients (except the food colouring) together.
2 Divide the mixture in two and add a few drops of red food colouring to one half. Mix thoroughly.
3 Shape the mixture into small squares.

Introduction
● Display and read the recipe for making Tudor gingerbread. Ask the children questions, such as: *What ingredients were put in these old-fashioned biscuits? How can we mix them? What shapes can they be?*
● Ask if they have had gingerbread before.

Main teaching activity
● Organise the children to work in pairs or small groups to make small amounts of gingerbread, colouring half the mixture with red food dye.
● Carefully cut the biscuits into squares and let the children arrange them on the plate with the cloves.
● Once made, let the children try the gingerbread or use the biscuits as part of the banqueting feast in the role-play area.

Plenary
● Discuss whether the children liked the gingerbread and talk about the reason for its name – because it was originally made with bread.
● Let the class try some modern gingerbread to compare.

Links
NLS Y1–2 Word level work: vocabulary extension by using words linked to a particular topic; Y2 T1 Text 13: to read simple recipes.

Differentiation
Less able readers will need support in reading the recipe. Encourage more able or older children to read the recipe out loud and to work more independently.

The lives of the people who worked in castles

Objectives
- To learn about people who used to live in castles.
- To learn about different ways of life in the past.
- To learn the vocabulary of chronology.

Vocabulary
breakfast, dinner, supper, bedtime

Resources
Pictures and stories of people from the past who could have worked in a castle; the photocopiable sheet 'A cook's day' on page 60.

Links
NLS Y1–2 Word level work: vocabulary extension by using words linked to a particular topic; Y2 T2 Text 13: to use story settings from reading, for example, re-describe, write a different story in the same setting.

Background
Life in a castle was very complex. Apart from the lord and his family, many people would have lived and worked there, such as the soldiers who guarded the walls, the servants and cooks. There would also have been people to look after the horses and mend their shoes, to repair and extend the castle, to grow food and farm the land. A castle would, in fact, have been more like an estate, supporting a great many local residents as well as those who lived inside its walls. As castles developed and became larger, the range of jobs they encompassed grew, involving many more domestic servants and people whose job was to look after the living quarters.

Introduction
- Tell the children that castles were huge buildings that were more than just homes for lords. Lots of people lived and worked there to defend the castle and to look after the lord and lady and their family.
- Talk about the different jobs that were done in castles and talk about the people who used to do them, such as soldiers, servants, cooks, blacksmiths and so on. If the children have already been to see a castle, ask them what they remember learning from the visit.
- Discuss how these sorts of jobs are done today.

Main teaching activity
- Read to the children the story on the photocopiable sheet 'A cook's day' on page 60. Discuss the story with the class, asking them questions, such as: *Do you think the cook enjoyed preparing the food for the Lord and Lady?*
- Then, as a shared writing lesson, work with the whole class to compile a short story about a day in the life of someone who lives in a castle, either a cook or another person.
- Let the children illustrate the story and create a display of their work.

Plenary
- Ask for volunteers to name the different types of work that had to be carried out in a castle. Talk about work that no longer needs to be done in castles today, such as blacksmiths to shoe horses or coopers to make water barrels. Encourage the children to think why this work is no longer necessary.

Differentiation
Care will be needed to ensure that ideas and suggestions are made from the whole ability range within the class for the story. More able writers might be encouraged to write their own short stories.

A hunting story

Objectives
● To find out about the past from stories.

Vocabulary
hunting, horses, hounds, hawks

Resources
The photocopiable sheet 'A hunting story' on page 61; pictures and other stories about hunting in the past; large sheet of paper for each child; coloured pens and pencils.

Background

This lesson focuses on the lives of the rich people who lived in castles. Hunting was a favourite pastime of royalty and the nobility for many hundreds of years. Known as the 'sport of kings', hunting was not only a sport, but also produced food for the table, in the form of game, such as deer, hares or wild boar. A wide variety of birds as well as dogs were used to help catch the prey, such as hawks and falcons. The lord and his immediate circle of friends or visitors would ride out from the castle on their horses to find large prey, such as deer or boar. They would be aided by other men with dogs, who would help to drive out animals from their hiding places in woodlands.

Falconry was a very specialised craft, involving the use of trained hawks, which would be launched from the hunter's arm to bring back birds, such as pigeons, for the table.

Introduction

● Introduce the subject of hunting by prompting the class with questions such as: *How did people who lived in castles get their food long ago? Did they get everything from the market? Where else could they find food? What was hunting like? What animals did they catch? Who would go hunting?*

Main teaching activity

● Talk about how one of the favourite activities of many kings and nobles was to go hunting. Tell the class how kings, like Henry VIII, and queens used to go hunting for deer and hares.
● Read the story from the photocopiable sheet on page 61 to the class.
● Give each child a piece of paper and show the children how to fold it into four to create a sequence of sections for them to draw and write in.
● Then ask the children to create a sequence of pictures and sentences or captions telling the story of the hunt, from the beginning, where the hunters leave the castle, to the final scene, where the food is being served in the Great Hall.

Plenary

● Ask for volunteers to show their hunting pictures or story sequences and to briefly retell their story to the rest of the class.

Links
NC English KS1: En1 (8a) telling stories, real and imagined.
NC Art and design KS1: (1a) to record from first-hand experience and imagination.

Differentiation

The less able children will need support with wordbanks and sentence construction. Encourage the more able children to write longer sentences below their pictures. Children in older age groups may also be able to extend their story beyond four scenes.

Heraldry

Background
From the Middle Ages, coats of arms have been used across Europe to symbolise important royal or noble family names, and also places. Their modern equivalent is the logo used by businesses and companies. Heraldic symbols were designed so that they could be 'read' and interpreted, for example: the *fleur-de-lis* represented the French monarchy, while the lion was used by English monarchs.

Introduction
● Show the class a selection of heraldic devices, and then focus on one large picture of a coat of arms. If possible, this should relate to the castle the children have visited, or to a local person or place. The school or town might have its own coat of arms.
● Look at the features of the coat of arms and discuss what each symbol means. Ask questions such as: *What is this called? What is a 'coat of arms'? What are symbols? What symbols can we find? What symbols could we invent for ourselves?*

Main teaching activity
● Talk about the children's names and ask them to think what symbols they might draw to represent these, for example: Smith might be represented by a hammer, Miller by a windmill and so on. Help all the children to devise symbols to represent their own names.
● Give out the blank outlines of shields and paints and colouring materials. Ask the children to draw their chosen symbols on the shield to make their own 'coat of arms'.
● Allow plenty of time for the children to create symbols to their own satisfaction and to complete their coats of arms.
● As they finish, encourage the children to consider if they are pleased with their work, or if they can think of any improvements they should make.
● Finally ask the children to write their own name in large print on the prepared labels.

Plenary
● Ask volunteers to show their coat of arms to the rest of the class and to explain the meaning of their chosen symbol.
● Together, make a class display of the finished shields, labelled with the children's names. Use some of the coats of arms inside the castle role-play area.

Differentiation
Less able children will need support in thinking up appropriate symbols for their coat of arms and adding detail to their drawings. The more able children in the class might be interested in looking up further heraldic symbols in reference books.

Sequencing castles

Objectives
● To place pictures of castles in chronological sequence.

Vocabulary
before, after, earlier, later

Resources
Variety of pictures showing forts and castles from two or three different times in the past (for example, Norman and Tudor); the photocopiable sheet 'Castles of the past' on page 62, one per child and one enlarged for display; narrow sheets of paper; large simple blank timeline for the classroom wall.

Background
Early Norman castles were built mainly for defence. They had very narrow window openings, so that arrows could be fired from them. Early castles were usually surrounded by a ditch or moat. The tallest part of the castle was the keep: a square or round tower built on top of a small hill or mound, which would make it more difficult to attack from below on foot. This resulted in a period in which warfare consisted mainly of sieges, where attackers surrounded castles, preventing any food or supplies from entering until the inhabitants surrendered, usually from starvation. In the late Middle Ages, castles continued to be important for defence and were built in a similar style, but they were larger and stronger than the earlier versions. Later Tudor castles were built more as grand aristocratic or royal residences, and had larger windows and bigger living quarters. They would be built on level ground, surrounded by formal ornamental gardens and substantial grounds.

Introduction
● Show the class a variety of pictures of castles that were built at different times.
● Discuss the key features of each one, such as size, building materials, shape of windows and so on.
● Talk about the differences in the castles. Ask the children questions, such as: *Which castle was built first? How can we tell?*

Main teaching activity
● Organise the children to work individually and give each child a copy of the photocopiable sheet 'Castles of the past' on page 62.
● Discuss the pictures briefly and identify together the features that show whether they are older or newer castles.
● Ask the children to sequence the pictures chronologically.
● Check the children's understanding as they work and ask them to explain why they have placed the pictures in a particular order.
● Ask the children to stick their pictures on narrow sheets of paper or in their books, in the correct sequence.

Plenary
● Ask for volunteers to place enlarged copies of the pictures in the right order on a simple timeline and give reasons for the order they decided on. Discuss how castles were built at different times, using the appropriate names for the periods, such as Norman and Tudor.

Differentiation
Less able children may need adult support in sorting out their sequences of pictures. Older or more able children may be able to write captions beneath each picture.

Links
NLS Y12 Word level work: vocabulary extension by using words linked to a particular topic.
NC English KS1: En1 (3) to join in a discussion as members of a group.

Cross-section of a home

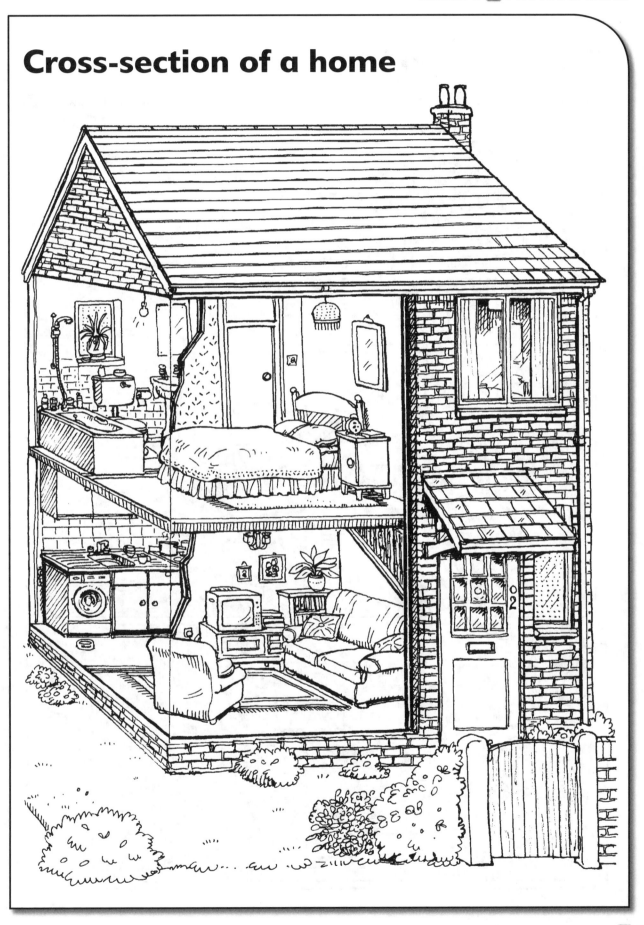

Cross-section of a castle keep

SCHOLASTIC

Menu for a meal in a castle

Leek and green pea soup

Freshly baked breads

Salmon

Roast boar

Roast suckling pig

Game pie

Syllabub

Poached pears in wine

Orange and lemon jumbles

Sweetmeats (marchpane, crystallised
fruits, gingerbread)

White and red wines

Ale

A cook's day

I work in the castle of my Lord and Lady. They are good noblefolk, but they do expect me to work very hard. I rise from my bed at three in the morning, for my Lord enjoys his bread freshly made each day. I have to make sure the scullery maid and my other kitchen helpers are ready for work too, and their first job is to fetch water from the well for cooking and cleaning, and to stoke up the big fire in the kitchen to get the ovens hot for the day's cooking. There is milk to bring in and churn into butter, vegetables to collect and wash and much baking to be done.

Once the bread is made I have to prepare my Lord's first meal. He likes plenty of cold meats and cheeses with his bread, and ale to wash it all down. He can then go out hunting with his hounds and horses. While he does this, I have to clear away and make sure the scullery maid cleans the table and platters. Then we have to begin preparing many different foods, such as soup, potage, pies and sweetmeats, for in the evening my Lord likes to entertain all his family and friends.

We trim the vegetables and prepare the fruits. We are having roast pigeons and pheasant today, and these all have to be plucked, washed and stuffed. The stuffing has to be mixed, and more fresh bread baked. My lord will also expect plenty of biscuits, pies and other sweetmeats to be ready when he has finished his pigeons. A cook's life is a busy one.

📖 S C H O L A S T I C

A hunting story

It was a bright sunny morning as we set off. I was on a small black mare that my father's friend, Lord Erwin, had found for me. We were visiting my Lord Erwin, because he was a great friend of my father's. They had fought together, side by side, in many battles.

I had been woken at about 4 o'clock that morning, and had to eat a small breakfast very quickly, so as not to miss the treat. My father had told me that we were off hunting boar, the small pigs that roamed wild in the forests in this part of the country.

I was enjoying the wild gallop down the hillside towards the woods, when I heard a loud horn sound from under the trees. Many men servants had gone on ahead, to beat the woods and frighten the boars out into the open, and I knew that this was the horn of the valet to my father.

Quickly we all chased towards the trees when, all of a sudden, there he was, the first wild boar I had chased, a fearsome sight if you had not been on horseback, eyes wild and angry and huge tusks ready to gore anyone who got in his way. He was certainly worth the chase, so off we went after him at full gallop.

He ran as wildly as he could, but was no match for the swift horse of my father, closely followed by the hounds that we had taken with us. In a moment, the boar was dead, speared through the heart. My father's valet was sounding his horn again to herald the event. I knew we would be having a good supper that night – roast boar!

Castles of the past

Norman castle

Medieval castle

Tudor castle

CHAPTER 4

Seaside holidays

This chapter supports Unit 4 'What were seaside holidays like in the past?' of the QCA Scheme of Work for History. The lesson plans focus on the seaside now, in the 1950s and the 1900s. With the popularity of beach holidays abroad, some children may have little experience of the UK seaside, so links with seaside holidays abroad can be made.

	OBJECTIVES	MAIN ACTIVITY
Lesson 1 P	To identify key features of seaside places. To distinguish between human and physical features. To find out about seaside places using a variety of sources.	Children consider the key aspects of modern seaside scenes, distinguishing between human and natural features.
Lesson 2 P	To find out about travel to the seaside in the past. To identify differences and similarities between travel to the seaside now and in the past. To gain some understanding of routes to the seaside.	The differences in travel to the seaside now and in the past are explored. The children learn about steam engines and day trips taken in the 1900s.
Lesson 3	To find out about the seaside resort's past by looking at buildings. To identify key features of the seaside through observation. To recognise that features are made by people or by nature.	Children visit a seaside resort and, in groups, explore different features, making sketches and notes and taking photographs.
Lesson 4 P	To place photographs in chronological order. To use vocabulary relating to the passage of time. To find out about the past using photographs. To identify similarities and differences between seaside holidays now and in the 1900s.	Sequencing an old and new photograph of a seaside resort helps the children to learn chronological order and to establish differences between past and present.
Lesson 5	To identify key features of seaside resorts in the 1900s. To find out about seaside resorts in the 1900s from a range of sources.	In groups, children research specific features of seaside resorts in the 1900s and record their findings in a poster format.
Lesson 6 P	To find out about paddle steamers using a variety of sources. To understand in simple terms how a paddle steamer works. To communicate their knowledge of a paddle-steamer trip through creating a storyboard.	Children learn about paddle steamers through photographs and listening to a story. They then label a picture and create a storyboard.
Lesson 7 P	To find out about seaside holidays in the past by listening to an eyewitness account. To ask the visitor questions about the past.	Children listen to a short talk from a visitor who remembers seaside holidays in the 1940s or 1950s and ask a range of prepared questions.
Lesson 8	To find out about seaside holidays by investigating souvenirs. To ask and answer questions about old historical objects. To talk about different seaside souvenirs and their purposes. To use everyday words and phrases to describe artefacts.	Looking at seaside souvenirs, including those from the past, leads children to create their own ribbon plate with a seaside scene.
Lesson 9	To find out what the seaside was like in the past. To communicate an understanding of the seaside in the past through art and craft activities. To communicate an understanding of seaside life using play.	Children create a seaside scene from the past, using art and craft materials, and use it for role play.
Lesson 10	To communicate their knowledge of seaside holidays in the past through role play. To find out about seaside holidays in the past using historical enquiry.	In groups and using a variety of reference material, children re-create and practise a seaside scene from the past for a role play.
Lesson 11	To find out what seaside resorts were like in the 1950s, using a range of resources. To identify some key features of holiday resorts in the 1950s. To introduce children to poetry about the seaside.	Children create a simple timeline and consider seaside resorts in the 1950s. They listen to a poem and then create shape poems of their own.
Lesson 12 P	To find out about seaside resorts in the past by looking at old postcards. To design and make their own postcard. To show the importance of postcards as a writing form.	Children look at old and new postcards and then create their own postcard – including the picture and a message.
Lesson 13	To know about the types of attractions at the UK seaside today. To understand why seaside holidays abroad are so popular. To communicate knowledge of seaside resorts today using text and images.	In groups children produce a poster showing the attractions of a particular seaside resort, referring to UK tourist brochures. They also list what they would like to see in resorts in the future.

What are seaside places?

Objectives
• To identify key features of seaside places.
• To distinguish between human and physical features.
• To find out about seaside places using a variety of sources.

Vocabulary
seaside, sand, rocks, beach, sea, pier, promenade, hotels, boats, human, natural

Resources
Enlarged photographs of the seaside; video material to show the seaside today; seaside resort website (a good starting point is www.visitbritain.com); large map; the photocopiable sheet 'What are seaside places?' on page 77, one per child; pre-prepared word cards of popular resorts (optional); blank word cards; poem about the seaside (some examples can be found in *Sea Dream: Poems From Under the Waves* compiled by Nikki Siegen-Smith (Barefoot Books) and *Read Me First: Younger Poems for Every Day of the Year* (Macmillan Children's Books, 2003).

Links
QCA Geography: Unit 4 'Going to the seaside'.

Background
This is a general introduction with a strong geographical focus. Children need to be able to recognise seaside features. Distinctions can be made at a simple level between what is natural and what has been made. Using the children's own experiences is clearly important, supplemented by good quality visual sources, such as the websites of popular resorts like Blackpool and Torquay.

Introduction
• Ask the children to talk about the places they have visited on holiday. Highlight the popularity of visiting the seaside, whether at home or abroad.
• Focus the discussion on UK seaside resorts, sharing with the children your own experiences of visits to the seaside.
• Show and discuss a large picture of a seaside resort, if possible using an interactive whiteboard and seaside resort website.

Main teaching activity
• Ask the children if they can name any seaside places in the UK that they have visited. Put the names on the board or use some pre-prepared word cards of popular resorts.
• Identify these places on a large map of the UK.
• Using a suitable video extract or photographs, show the children some seaside scenes. Ask them to identify key features like the sea, beach, rocks, sand, pier, promenade and hotels.
• Discuss the idea that some of these things are natural and others have been made by people. Can the children give any examples of natural features and those made by humans?
• Ask the children to identify a few reasons why people visit the seaside. Emphasise attractions like the beach, sea views and the opportunity for relaxation.
• Give each child a copy of the photocopiable sheet 'What are seaside places?' on page 77. Ask the children to label the main features and sort a few of them into human and natural categories.

Plenary
• Ask the children to say what seaside features they have found in the picture. Can they give any examples made by people or made by nature? Conclude the lesson by reading a short story or poem about the seaside that reinforces key seaside features.

Differentiation
Children will need support to avoid misconceptions over human and natural features. Simplify the language as necessary. More able children can be expected to write extended sentences about the reasons for visiting the seaside.

Travel to the seaside now and then

Objectives
● To find out about travel to the seaside in the past.
● To identify differences and similarities between travel to the seaside now and in the past.
● To gain some understanding of routes to the seaside.

Vocabulary
smoke, coal, steam train, railway station, platform, railway carriage, day trip

Resources
Photographs and video material of old trains; photographs of cars by the seaside today; map; the photocopiable sheet 'Travel to the seaside' on page 78; websites such as the National Railway Museum (www.nrm.org.uk).

Links
QCA Geography: Unit 4 'Going to the seaside'.
QCA Science: Unit 2E 'Forces and movement'.

Background
Before the 1840s, seaside resorts existed but were the preserve of the middle and upper classes. The coming of the railway made the seaside accessible for the masses, if only for day trips. These were encouraged by the Bank Holiday Act of 1871, which introduced public holidays and led to the popularity of the bank holiday rail excursion to the seaside. Resorts like Blackpool, Scarborough and Skegness saw considerable expansion as a result. Rail travel to the seaside remained significant until the mass ownership of cars in the 1960s. Railways in the 1900s were operated by steam locomotives.

Introduction
● Ask the children how they have travelled to the seaside. Emphasise the importance of the car, supporting this by a relevant photograph.
● On a map, show the nearest seaside resort(s) to the school and a possible route. Highlight some of the key places on the journey.
● Then ask the children to think about how people travelled to the seaside a long time ago before we had cars. Emphasise the importance of rail travel and display a relevant photograph.

Main teaching activity
● Look at photographs or video material showing trains in the 1900s.
● Discuss what the trains looked like in the past. Can the children identify the steam engine pulling the carriages?
● Point out the steam and smoke. Ask the children to explain in simple terms how the steam engine works. Clarify the use of coal, which is burned to heat water and to make steam - reference to how a kettle works might be useful here.
● Tell the children how the building of railways allowed large numbers of people to visit seaside places like Blackpool and Brighton.
● Many of these people came only for a day trip. Ask why they only stayed one day. Encourage suggestions that most people did not have the money and were not paid if they went on holiday.
● Give out the photocopiable sheet 'Travel to the seaside' on page 78 for the children to complete.

Plenary
● Discuss the children's responses on the photocopiable sheet. Conclude by asking them to summarise the key differences between travel to the seaside in the 1900s and today.

Differentiation
Word cards will help the less able children. More able children could write a few sentences about travel to the seaside.

Visit to the seaside

Objectives
- To find out about the seaside resort's past by looking at buildings.
- To identify key features of the seaside through observation.
- To recognise that features are made by people or by nature.

Vocabulary
beach, promenade, pier, sea, hotels

Resources
Materials for sketching and taking notes; old photographs of the resort (a set for each small group); local tourist information brochures; disposable cameras (optional); old and current OS maps of the resort (optional).

Links
QCA Geography: Unit 4 'Going to the seaside'.

Background
A visit to a seaside resort would be beneficial to this topic, particularly if the children's experiences of the seaside might be limited. Careful attention needs to be given to the organisation of the visit. Adult helpers are essential and they must be thoroughly briefed. You need to comply with LEA risk assessment rules, and clarify practical arrangements, such as toilets and wet weather contingencies.

Organise a walking route that is safe, compact and introduces children to important seaside features, such as the beach, promenade and pier. An alternative to a field trip would be to focus on a single resort in the classroom, making use of tourist information resources and the resort's website, if it is appropriate.

Introduction
- On arrival at the seaside, gather the class together to focus their attention on the purpose of the visit.

Main teaching activity
- Explore key features of the seaside resort, such as the promenade, beach, hotels and pier. Ask the children what they can see, hear and even smell at the seaside. Encourage them to observe and to ask questions about what they can see.
- Show the children a few old photographs of the seaside resort. Find where one of the photographs was taken from and compare past and present views. Take a photograph of the view today for later use.
- Allow the children to make brief notes and sketches. Provide them with disposable cameras to use. They could have a list of things found at the seaside to tick or you can play an 'I spy' game.
- Look at some of the buildings. Discuss what the buildings are and what they are used for. Are they old? How can the children tell? Point out that old buildings can tell us what a place was like in the past.

Plenary
- Share what the children have seen and found out. Ask them why they think the place is a popular seaside resort.
- Interesting follow-up classroom activities can be developed, such as creating a guide to the resort using ICT.
- Comparing old and modern large-scale OS maps of the resort would also be useful to show geographical features and change over time.

Differentiation
Adult group leaders may need to give children help with the drawing and sketching. Less able children may need more prompting to closely observe their surroundings. More able children will be able to write more detailed notes.

Photographs of seaside resorts

Objectives
● To place photographs in chronological order.
● To use vocabulary relating to the passage of time.
● To find out about the past using photographs.
● To identify similarities and differences between seaside holidays now and in the 1900s.

Vocabulary
similar, different, 1900s, old, modern

Resources
Photographs of a seaside scene in the 1900s and the same or similar scene in the present day; the photocopiable sheet 'Comparing seaside holidays in the 1900s and today' on page 79, one per child; string and pegs; cards – one reading '1900', one reading the current year.

Links
NLS Y1 T3 Text 22: to record answers, for example, as lists; Y2 T3 Text 21: to write simple non-chronological reports. QCA Geography: Unit 4 'Going to the seaside'.

Background
Sequencing photographs and using a simple timeline are useful strategies to develop chronological understanding at KS1 level. Encourage children to look carefully at the pictures and give them opportunities to discuss issues like similarities and differences.

Introduction
● Start the lesson by asking the children to think about ways of finding out about seaside holidays in the past, such as the use of reference books. Write a few suggestions on the board.
● Highlight the importance of photographs by introducing the 1900s scene and discuss what clues indicate that it is an old photograph. Explain that they will be looking at this photograph and comparing it with a modern one in order to see how the place has changed.

Main teaching activity
● Display the modern-day photograph alongside the example from the 1900s. Discuss both the scenes and encourage the children to say which looks the oldest and which the most modern and why.
● Using string and pegs, create a simple timeline and ask for volunteers to put the photographs in chronological order and to add two date cards, one for 1900 and one for the current year. Can they work out how many years there are between the two photographs?
● Compare the features of both photographs, such as the way people are dressed, transport, the pier and beach activities. What similarities can the children see? What differences are there?
● Give the children a copy each of the photocopiable sheet 'Comparing seaside holidays in the 1900s and today' on page 79 and ask them to complete the activities.

Plenary
● Once all the children have completed their photocopiable sheets, review the children's answers together. Ask children to explain the reasons for their decisions.
● With the children's help, list on the board any similarities and differences between the pictures. Emphasise how over the years some things change but others remain the same.

Differentiation
Ensure that less able children are clearly aware which scene is old and which is new. You may need to simplify vocabulary according to individual children's level of ability. The timeline activity could be made more challenging for more able children by introducing photographs from other periods such as the 1950s.

The seaside in the 1900s

Objectives
● To identify key features of seaside resorts in the 1900s.
● To find out about seaside resorts in the 1900s from a range of sources.

Vocabulary
beach, pier, promenade, bathing machines, hotels

Resources
Video extract on the seaside in the 1900s; group resource pack, including photographs and reference books on features, such as the pier and beach; topic question cards; large sheets of paper; writing and drawing materials; sample information poster; computers (optional).

Links
NLS Y1 T3 Text 21: to use the language and features of non-fiction texts to make class books; Y2 T3 Text 20: to write non-fiction texts using a given model.
QCA ICT: Unit 2B 'Creating pictures'.
QCA Geography: Unit 4 'Going to the seaside'.

Background
The 1900s were a prosperous and busy period for seaside resorts before the onset of the First World War. The availability of good quality photographic evidence for this period makes it a very worthwhile focus of study. Photographs show how popular walking along the promenade was, and piers also attracted many people with boat trips, shows and various amusements. Photographic evidence can be supplemented by a useful collection of readily available educational reference books about seaside holidays that are KS1 orientated.

Introduction
● Tell the children that they will be looking at a video extract of the seaside in the 1900s. Ask them to watch very carefully and to focus on the seaside scenes and activities shown.
● Discuss the video and encourage the children to identify features, such as the beach, pier, hotels and promenade. Put these names on the board or use word cards.
● Tell the children that they will be working in groups to find out about one of these topics in more detail and to produce a poster.

Main teaching activity
● Split the class into groups, allocating a seaside feature to each one. Ask the groups to investigate their topic, using the photographs and reference books provided.
● Structure the research by giving the children question cards for each topic, such as: *What does a pier look like? What is it made of? What was a pier used for? What was found on the pier?*
● Ask each group to produce a large information poster about the feature, using text in bullet form and some drawings. This could be a simple flipchart poster or a more elaborate piece for display purposes. ICT could be used to support this activity.
● Show the children an example of an information poster so they have a model for their own task.
● Groups will need to be carefully monitored and supported during this research activity.

Plenary
● Bring the class together and allow each group to talk about what they have found out, using their poster. Posters could be combined to produce a guide to the seaside resort in the 1900s.

Differentiation
Arrange the children in mixed-ability groups for this poster activity which requires a range of skills. Careful teacher support will need to be given to individual groups to ensure that investigations and poster work are focused.

A trip on a paddle steamer

Objectives
● To find out about paddle steamers using a variety of sources.
● To understand in simple terms how a paddle steamer works.
● To communicate their knowledge of a paddle-steamer trip through creating a storyboard.

Vocabulary
paddle steamer, pier, funnel, flag, paddle wheel, mast

Resources
Enlarged photographs of a paddle steamer (moored at a pier and a variety of general and close-up views); appropriate websites or published resources about paddle steamers; the photocopiable sheet 'A trip on a paddle steamer' on page 80, one per child.

Links
NLS Y2 T3 Text 10: to write sustained stories.
QCA Science: Unit 2E 'Forces and movement'.
NC Science KS1: Sc3 (1d) to find out about the uses of a variety of materials and how these are chosen for specific uses on the basis of their simple properties.

Background
Paddle steamers were a distinctive part of seaside resorts from the Victorian period until the 1960s. They provided a popular opportunity for pleasure cruises but also, particularly before the First World War, operated important passenger services to resorts such as Llandudno. Today a restored paddle steamer called Waverley continues to sail from many piers around the UK. Useful websites that can support this lesson include the National Piers Society (www.piers.co.uk).

Introduction
● Show the children an enlarged picture of a seaside pier with a paddle steamer moored at the end.
● Using a storytelling format, talk about walking down the pier to buy a ticket at the end. Explain why you need a ticket. Focus on the boat and explain that this is called a paddle steamer.
● Introduce a close-up photograph of the paddle steamer. Tell the children that they are about to have a trip on a paddle steamer.

Main teaching activity
● Tell a story of boarding the steamer and leaving the pier, using appropriate pictures. For example: *You buy your ticket and board the steamer. Soon the boat is ready to leave, its whistle sounds, the ropes are cast off, and clouds of black smoke come out of the funnel and then the steamer is speeding away.*
● Use further pictures to look at the features of the boat. Talk about how paddle wheels make it move. Explain that the engines were powered by steam. Look at the boats on deck. Why were they there?
● Talk about reasons why a boat trip is enjoyable, such as the open sea, the fresh air, and the coastal scenery. Ask the children how a paddle-steamer trip might not be very pleasant.
● Give each child a copy of the photocopiable sheet on page 80 and ask them to label the picture of the paddle steamer. Then ask them to make some suggestions for a story about a trip on a paddle steamer. They can produce a short storyboard using their own pictures and some of the words provided.

Plenary
● Read out some of the children's stories.
● Conclude by talking about a paddle steamer called Waverley, which is the world's last sea-going paddle steamer and still runs trips from UK seaside resorts.

Differentiation
Additional words and phrases could be provided to aid their writing. Consider mixed-ability groups for shared writing. Some children might need the activity to be presented in a sentence completion format.

Talking about seaside holidays in the past

Objectives
● To find out about seaside holidays in the past by listening to an eyewitness account.
● To ask the visitor questions about the past.

Vocabulary
oral history, memory, souvenir, holiday, photographs

Resources
Artefacts and seaside holiday photographs brought in by the visitor; reference books (including Big Books) about the seaside and life after the Second World War; the photocopiable sheet 'Seaside holidays' on page 81, one per child.

Background
Oral history has much to contribute to classroom history. Careful preparation is needed to ensure the success of such a session. It should be possible to find a local person who can talk about seaside holidays in the 1940s or 1950s when they were a child. One of the children's grandparents might be a possibility. The visitor needs to be briefed about the session, but it is important to be flexible. Encourage the visitor to bring in artefacts or photographs. A Big Book on seaside holidays might also be a useful resource.

Introduction
● Ask the children how we can find out what seaside holidays were like in the past. Write key words on the board, such as: books, photographs and objects. Guide the children to identify the value of talking with older people about what their holidays were like when they were children. Introduce the term 'oral history'.
● Explain that a visitor is coming to talk about seaside holidays in the past and to answer their questions. Draw up a list of questions that they could ask the visitor. See the photocopiable sheet 'Seaside holidays' on page 81 for an example of appropriate questions.

Main teaching activity
● Introduce the visitor to the children. The lesson format might vary according to the wishes of the visitor, but typically it will consist of an initial short talk followed by questions from the children. The inclusion of souvenirs and photographs would be helpful.
● Encourage the children to listen carefully and politely to the visitor, and to record some answers to their questions in both written and picture forms. Key points could be displayed on the board.

Plenary
● Review the children's understanding by asking them what they have found out about seaside holidays in the past. Give children an opportunity to ask any final questions.
● Conclude by giving a copy of the photocopiable sheet 'Seaside holidays' on page 81 to each child for them to interview their own parents, carers or grandparents. The information produced can provide discussion opportunities in a subsequent session and can be summarised in chart form, using bullet points.

Differentiation
Monitor the vocabulary used by the visitor to ensure that it matches the children's language levels. Discuss unfamiliar words with them. The less able will need support in writing up the interview.

Links
QCA Citizenship: Unit 1 'Taking part'.
NC English KS1: En1 (1) to speak clearly and with confidence; (2) to listen and respond to others.

Investigating seaside souvenirs

Objectives
- To find out about seaside holidays by investigating souvenirs.
- To ask and answer questions about old historical objects.
- To talk about different seaside souvenirs and their purposes.
- To use everyday words and phrases to describe artefacts.

Vocabulary
souvenir, ribbon plate, rim, photographs, postcards, rock

Resources
Collection of modern seaside souvenirs; examples of old souvenirs, such as a ribbon plate and other china items (use photographs if real artefacts are not available); cardboard plates; drawing and painting materials; completed cardboard example of a ribbon plate; reference books and pictures of seaside resorts.

Links
NC Art and design KS1: (2b) to try out tools and techniques and apply these to materials and processes, including drawing; (2c) to design and make images and artefacts.

Background
A popular late Victorian souvenir was the ribbon plate. It was a plate with holes on the outer rim that could be intertwined with a ribbon and, in the centre, there was usually a scene of the seaside resort. Mass production means that many have survived and can be found relatively cheaply.

Introduction
- Show the children a collection of modern seaside souvenirs. Ask them to identify the objects and their link with the seaside. Introduce the word 'souvenir' and its meaning (French for 'to remember').
- Discuss why we buy souvenirs.
- Tell the children that in the lesson they will be looking at seaside souvenirs from a long time ago.

Main teaching activity
- Introduce a few old seaside souvenirs to the class, asking the children to identify them.
- Focus on the ribbon plate. Encourage the children to ask and answer questions about it. What shape is it? What is it made from? What does the picture show? What would it have been used for? Why are there holes on the edge of the plate?
- Record their observations on the board, explaining that this is a seaside souvenir called a ribbon plate. Show how a ribbon could be attached round the edge of the plate.
- Emphasise that ribbon plates were very popular in the 1900s and were bought as ornaments.
- Say that they are going to make their own ribbon plate and show them your completed example. Explain how it was made using a cardboard plate.
- Using appropriate reference sources, children can choose a seaside resort, draw a picture and write a caption such as: *A present from Blackpool*. The edges can also be decorated to imitate the ribbon.

Plenary
- Review progress made by the children. Ask for volunteers to say which seaside resort they have chosen and what their picture shows.
- Conclude by emphasising how souvenirs like ribbon plates can tell us what a seaside resort looked like in the past.

Differentiation
Less able children may need support with the initial research to help them identify a specific seaside resort and choose a suitable scene. Some children may need help with the layout of their plate.

A seaside play area

Objectives
● To find out what the seaside was like in the past.
● To communicate an understanding of the seaside in the past through art and craft activities.
● To communicate an understanding of seaside life using play.

Vocabulary
beach, sea, sand, pier, promenade

Resources
Variety of art and craft resources, such as cardboard and modelling materials; reference books; photographs or video clip; costumes.

Links
NC Art and design: (2b) to try out tools and techniques and apply these to materials and processes, including drawing; (2c) to design and make images and artefacts.

Background
Children's understanding of the seaside in the past can be enhanced by creating a seaside scene in a classroom corner. There are many possibilities for this, such as choosing a particular period like the 1900s or 1950s or focusing on individual themes, such as the pier or the beach. Artefacts, particularly from more recent times, can often be sourced from parents and the local museum education service might also be able to provide a collection.

Introduction
● Explain to the children they will be helping to create a seaside scene from the past, such as the 1900s, in the classroom.
● Show the children enlarged photographs or a short video clip as a stimulus for ideas. Ask the children to identify some features that they could incorporate into their seaside scene.
● List these ideas and, with the children's help, draw up a plan.

Main teaching activity
● Discuss the tasks that need to be done to create a seaside scene.
● Organise the children to work in groups or individually, depending on the nature of the activity. These might include:
    ● making a Punch and Judy show theatre out of cardboard and decorating it
    ● collecting seaside souvenirs, organising them into a museum display and writing captions (or replicas could be made or drawn)
    ● creating a model of a seaside resort to include features like the promenade, beach, pier and beach huts
    ● producing a wall frieze of a seaside scene.
● Give the children plenty of opportunities to research what they are creating and make reference books and photographs available.
● Once the scene is completed, let the children use it actively, including talking about the display and engaging in role play, preferably using costumes.

Plenary
● The nature of this activity does not necessarily fit into the time or structure of a formal lesson and may need to be carried over into subsequent sessions. Nevertheless it is important for progress to be reviewed. Encourage the children to talk about their work and what they have found out about seaside holidays.

Differentiation
Children will need careful support and guidance with this work. Given the strong emphasis on practical art and craft activities, extra assistance from adult helpers would be invaluable. Mixed-ability groups would be preferable, allowing the children to share their skills.

A seaside role play

Objectives
● To communicate their knowledge of seaside holidays in the past through role play.
● To find out about seaside holidays in the past using historical enquiry.

Vocabulary
pier, bathing machines, promenade, Punch and Judy, beach, camera, photograph, sand, donkey

Resources
Enlarged photographs of seaside scenes from the 1900s or a schools video programme; list of seaside scenes; reference books; group task cards; costumes.

Links
NC English KS1: En1 (1) to speak clearly and with confidence; (2) to listen and respond to others; (3) to join in as members of a group; (4b) to create and sustain roles.
S&L Y2 T1: Drama: adopt appropriate roles in small or large groups.

Background
Role play and drama is generally enjoyed by children and positively commented upon by Ofsted. Structured role play in history can help promote empathy, imagination and allow children to actively re-create the past. Effective role play, however, should be underpinned by careful historical enquiry based on children gaining knowledge of the issue by using resources such as stories, television, photographs, reference books or the internet.

Introduction
● Show the children some examples of different seaside scenes from, for example, the 1900s, using enlarged photographs or a schools video programme on seaside holidays; ensure these stimuli include some drama activities, for example, people walking on the promenade, having their photograph taken or buying an ice-cream.
● Ask the children what is taking place, where and who is involved. Are any artefacts being used? What might the people be saying?
● Explain to the children that they will be working in groups to create their own role play about the seaside in the past.

Main teaching activity
● Give the children examples of seaside scenes that the groups are to focus upon, such as visiting the pier, playing on the beach and walking on the promenade.
● Take one of these scenes and use a photograph to discuss what is happening. Ask the children what they might do to re-create the scene. Discuss the different roles of the people involved and what they might say. Encourage the children to think about actions, artefacts and costumes that could be used.
● Explain that each group will have a photograph, reference book and task card to help them with the activity.
● Split the class into groups allocating them a seaside scene. Give support to each group, ensuring that they discuss the scene carefully and plan out a simple role play in which all members participate.
● Children will need an opportunity to practise their role play and groups will clearly benefit from close support, including the teacher actually modelling conversations and actions from their scene.

Plenary
● Groups can present their role play to the rest of the class. Encourage the children to think about what each role play shows about seaside holidays in the past.

Differentiation
Mixed-ability groups will be useful with this activity, allowing children to pool their skills and support each other.

The seaside in the 1950s

Objectives
● To find out what seaside resorts were like in the 1950s, using a range of resources.
● To identify some key features of holiday resorts in the 1950s.
● To introduce children to poetry about the seaside.

Vocabulary
caravan, holiday camp, amusement arcade deckchairs

Resources
Timeline materials (string, pegs, labels for '1900s', '1950s' and 'today'); photographs of seaside holidays in the 1900s, 1950s and today, preferably of the same resort and similar view; paper and pens; computers (optional); word cards; poem about the seaside, for example: 'The Sandcastle' by John Foster from *See You Later Escalator: Rhymes for the Very Young* chosen by John Foster (Oxford University Press).

Links
NLS Y1 T3 Text 15: to use poems as models for own writing; Y2 T1 Text 12: to use simple poetry structures; Y2 T2 Text 15: to use structures from poems as a basis for writing.
NC English KS1: En3 (1a) to use adventurous and wide-ranging vocabulary.

Background
In the 1950s relative prosperity followed a period of post-war austerity. Wages and employment levels rose, which enabled people to have more holidays. Although often physically neglected, popular resorts attracted vast numbers of people. Rail excursions brought many visitors, but car travel was becoming increasingly important. Bank holiday traffic problems became common. Changes in accommodation patterns were noticeable with the expansion of caravans and holiday camps like Butlin's. Photographs of the seaside in the 1950s often show busy beaches with adults relaxing in deckchairs and children playing in the sand.

Introduction
● Show children a simple timeline highlighting the 1900s, 1950s and today. Ask them to match the appropriate seaside picture to the dates. Invite them to say how the seaside has changed over these different periods.
● Emphasise that the lesson will explore the 1950s. Using the timeline, ask the children how many years ago this was.

Main teaching activity
● Use a range of sources, such as photographs, to highlight what seaside holidays were like in the 1950s. Ask the children to identify typical features or activities and record these on the board or use word cards. Discussions might include references to caravans, holiday parks, deckchairs, donkeys, Punch and Judy shows, boat trips, ice-cream sellers, and beach activities, such as paddling.
● Introduce a poem about the seaside, such as 'The Sandcastle' by John Foster. Discuss the meaning of the poem and the words used.
● Take one of the seaside features of the 1950s previously identified, such as a boat trip, and write a few verses for a poem about this with the children. Draw a shape to represent the boat and show how the poem could be fitted into this.
● Encourage the children to write their own shape poems about the seaside in the 1950s. ICT could be effectively used with this activity.

Plenary
● Ask for volunteers to read out their poems. Use these examples to summarise some of the main features of seaside holidays in the 1950s.

Differentiation
Word cards will be an essential reference point for this activity. Individual support, particularly for less able children, will be needed when drafting poems. The more able should be encouraged to develop their poems. Assistance may be needed with drawing the shapes.

Postcards

Objectives
● To find out about seaside resorts in the past by looking at old postcards.
● To design and make their own postcard.
● To show the importance of postcards as a writing form.

Vocabulary
older, oldest, newer, postcard, post office, stamp, postmark, address, message

Resources
Examples of modern postcards; old postcards, photocopied for the children and one enlarged for display; the photocopiable sheet 'Postcards' on page 82, one per child; reference books; photographs; drawing materials.

Links
NLS Y1 T3 Text 20: to write simple recounts linked to topics of interest or to personal experience; Y2 T1 Text 11: to use language of time to structure a sequence of events.

Background
The British Post Office approved the use of postcards with the address and message on one side in 1902. Ever since they have become a major part of seaside tradition. Postcards provide an invaluable source for old photographs of seaside resorts. Both originals and modern reproductions can be obtained relatively easily. A collectors' fair can be a useful source for old postcards. Apart from traditional seaside scenes, comic cards are an integral part of postcard culture and first appeared about 1905. Given careful choice, this type of postcard will generate interesting discussion.

Introduction
● Show the children examples of present day seaside postcards that have been posted. Allow them to handle and look at them carefully. Have they ever sent or received postcards?
● Emphasise that postcards have been used for a long time and that they can tell us important information about seaside holidays.

Main teaching activity
● Give the children a photocopy of an old postcard (preferably from the 1950s) and ask them to look at it carefully. An enlarged copy of this would also be useful to refer to.
● Ask the children to talk about different parts of the postcard, for example: *What does the picture show? Which seaside resort is it? What picture is on the stamp? Is there a postmark showing the date when the postcard was posted? What does the address say? Is there a message?* Compile a list on the board of the key parts of a postcard.
● Give the children a copy each of the photocopiable sheet 'Postcards' on page 82. Explain to the children that they are to make their own postcard. Emphasise that they will need to draw a seaside scene, write a message and address it. Reference books and photographs need to be made available to stimulate ideas.
● Discuss what they could put in the message, such as references to weather, places visited and how they are enjoying the holiday. Put examples on the board and ensure that a wordbank is clearly visible.

Plenary
● Review the children's work, looking at their pictures and writing. Point out that seaside postcards do not just have pictures of the local area but there are also funny cartoon-style examples to make people laugh. Conclude by showing an example and briefly discussing it.

Differentiation
The more able children should be encouraged to draft and revise their messages. Focused support by the teacher will be needed for less able children working on the written task.

Seaside holidays today

Objectives
- To know about the types of attractions at the UK seaside today.
- To understand why seaside holidays abroad are so popular.
- To communicate knowledge of seaside resorts today using text and images.

Vocabulary
abroad, Spain, Europe, aircraft, travel brochure

Resources
Maps to show seaside resorts in the UK and Europe, package tour brochures, tourist information for UK seaside resorts; large sheets of paper; pens and drawing materials.

Background
While primarily looking at UK seaside resorts, this final session also initially explores the popularity of foreign holidays. It also gives children an opportunity to say what they think seaside resorts should offer in the future, emphasising that these places are continuously changing to meet visitors' needs.

Introduction
- Start by carrying out a quick class survey to find out where the children have been on recent seaside holidays.
- Highlight the popularity today of families going on seaside holidays abroad to countries like Spain. Emphasise this point by showing children some travel brochures and locating popular European beach destinations on a map of Europe.
- Briefly explore reasons for the growth of foreign seaside holidays, such as poor weather in the UK, the growth of air travel and the low cost of package holidays.
- Nevertheless, emphasise that the UK seaside is still very popular and this session will explore its attractions.

Main teaching activity
- Divide the class into groups and provide each one with a tourist brochure and information about one resort.
- Explain how a tourist brochure tries to encourage visitors by showing the attractions of the resort.
- Ask the children to look through their information to find out the name of the resort and what is of interest there.
- Hand out large sheets of paper, pens and drawing material. Ask the groups to produce a poster to show the attractions of their resort, using both text and pictures.
- Once they have finished, invite the children to think of attractions they would like to see in seaside resorts to encourage visitors in the future. Ask them to make a list, either in words or illustrations, of some of their ideas.

Plenary
- Groups can share posters with the rest of the class and talk about their chosen seaside resort.
- Finally ask the groups to present their suggestions for attractions that they would like to see in seaside resorts in the future.

Links
NLS Y2 T3 Text 21: to write non-chronological reports.
QCA Geography: Unit 4 'Going to the seaside'.

Differentiation
Mixed-ability grouping is recommended here, but monitor groups carefully to ensure the active participation of all the children. Groups will need support with the research and poster layout. Encourage them to divide tasks amongst themselves.

What are seaside places?

◧ Look at this seaside picture. Colour in the things that are named in the wordbank. Draw a line from the word to the correct part of the picture.

| beach pier hotels promenade rocks sand sea boat |

◧ Write two things in the picture that have been made by people.

_____   _____

◧ List two things in the picture that have not been made by people.

_____   _____

◧ Complete this sentence:

People visit the seaside because _____

_____

_____

Travel to the seaside

In this picture people are arriving by train at a seaside town in the 1900s.

◼ Write some of the things that you can see in this picture.

_____   _____   _____

_____   _____   _____

Here are some facts about how people travelled to the seaside a long time ago in the 1900s.

◼ In the 1900s most people travelled to the seaside on the railways.

◼ The people sat in railway carriages. A steam engine at the front of the train pulled the carriages along.

◼ Many people went to the seaside to visit for only one day.

◼ On the back of this sheet, draw a picture to show how you travel to the seaside today.

Comparing seaside holidays in the 1900s and today

Which seaside picture is from a long time ago (1900s) and which shows the seaside today (now)? Put these dates in the correct boxes below.

■ What is different between the seaside of the 1900s and the seaside of today? What is the same?

■ Record your answers on the back of this sheet in a table like this:

Differences	Similarities

A trip on a paddle steamer

◀ Draw a line to match words in the wordbank to the things that you see in this picture of a paddle steamer.

| funnel | mast | paddle box | lifeboat | flag | paddle wheel | passengers | anchor |

◀ Draw a storyboard of a trip on a paddle steamer on the back of this sheet or in your book. Use the words below to help you.

the paddle steamer leaves the pier	the blue sea	seagulls flying
the lighthouse	black smoke from the funnel	the boat arrives back at the pier

Seaside holidays

■ Talk with an older person, such as a parent or grandparent, about their seaside holiday when they were a child. Here are some questions for you to ask and spaces to write the answers.

Which seaside places did you go to on holiday as a child?

_____

About how many years ago was this?

_____

Who did you go with?

_____

How did you travel there?

_____

What did you do at the seaside?

_____

_____

_____

What happy memories do you have of seaside holidays as a child?

_____

_____

What souvenirs did you bring back from your holidays?

_____

_____

Postcards

◼ Draw a seaside picture for your postcard. Fill in the name of the seaside resort.

◼ Now write a short message to a friend about what you have been doing on holiday and fill in the address.

Dear

Address:

_____

_____

_____

_____

_____

1st

CHAPTER 5

Florence Nightingale

This chapter focuses on the life of Florence Nightingale, who is famed for her efforts to treat sick and wounded servicemen during the Crimean War and for her role in helping to establish nursing as a profession. In addition, two lessons focus on Mary Seacole as a comparison. She was also a nurse (of Jamaican origin) from England, but she travelled to the Crimea on her own accord. This is an opportunity to look at the contribution of people from minority groups in the history of Britain.

The photocopiable resources in this chapter provide information on the lives of these two nurses for the teacher to read out or to adapt to a suitable level for the children.

	OBJECTIVES	MAIN ACTIVITY
Lesson 1	To find out about the past from pictures and photographs.	Children look at pictures of Florence Nightingale, discuss her life and work, and then draw portraits.
Lesson 2 P	To find out about the past from written sources. To communicate their knowledge of history in a variety of ways.	Children read a story together about Florence Nightingale, answer questions and pick out key words.
Lesson 3 P	To find out about the past from visual sources. To recognise similarities and differences between being a nurse today and a long time ago.	Pictures of Florence Nightingale and a modern nurse are compared and children complete a matching activity.
Lesson 4 P	To understand why Florence Nightingale acted as she did. To locate the site of a historical event on a map or globe.	Children locate the Crimea on a globe and use a map to plot the journey Florence Nightingale would have taken.
Lesson 5	To find out about the past from oral sources.	Children listen to a recording of Florence Nightingale speaking.
Lesson 6	To find out about the past from role play and drama.	A hot-seating activity allows the children to ask Florence Nightingale prepared questions.
Lesson 7 P	To communicate historical knowledge through drama.	Children practise and role play key events from Florence Nightingale's life.
Lesson 8 P	To find out about the past from first-hand written sources. To understand that the past is represented in different ways.	Listening to accounts from two nurses in the Crimea lets the children consider alternative viewpoints. They then create a short story in shared writing.
Lesson 9	To communicate their learning about hospitals and nursing through role play. To apply their knowledge and understanding of hospitals and nursing a long time ago.	Children set up an area to represent a ward in the Scutari hospital and use it for role play to reinforce learning and for assessment purposes.
Lesson 10 P	To sequence the events in Florence Nightingale's life.	Children order sentences detailing key events in Florence Nightingale's life and then draw a picture sequence.
Lesson 11 P	To recap what they have learned about Florence Nightingale.	Completing a grid with information about Florence Nightingale allows the children to reflect on their learning.
Lesson 12	To communicate their knowledge of history in a variety of ways.	Children prepare and rehearse in groups before holding an assembly.
Lesson 13	To find out about the past from pictures and photographs.	Children learn about Mary Seacole and draw a picture sequence of her life and work.
Lesson 14 P	To find out about the past from written sources. To communicate their knowledge of history in a variety of ways.	Children listen to an extract from Mary Seacole's autobiography and select words for a wordbank.

Florence Nightingale

Objectives
● To find out about the past from pictures and photographs.

Vocabulary
famous person, nurse, war, soldiers

Resources
Enlarged pictures and photographs of Florence Nightingale at different times in her life; globe or map of the world; drawing or painting materials and paper.

Background

Florence Nightingale was named after the town of Florence, in Italy, where she was born on 12 May 1820. At the age of 34, when the Crimean War broke out, she was sent by the government to work as a nurse at Scutari in Turkey, an army hospital for the soldiers in the war, along with 38 nurses she had enlisted. She had already spent much of her adult life working as a nurse, sometimes against the wishes of her parents. She maintained a very religious outlook on life, and believed that she had been called by God to do His will. Florence's family, who were quite well off, could never understand Florence's need to work, especially in a profession that was, at the time, so often associated with terrible conditions.

Introduction

● Tell the children that they are going to learn about a famous person from long ago, called Florence Nightingale.
● Ask who has heard about her before. Prompt the children with question such as: *Who has heard of Florence Nightingale? Why is she so famous? What did she do? How do we know? Why do you think we still remember her today?*

Main teaching activity

● Show the class a selection of enlarged pictures and photographs of Florence Nightingale at different times in her life.
● Describe a little about her life and work – or ask any of the children to tell you what they know already.
● Ask the children if they can guess what she was like as a person from looking at the pictures.
● Discuss why we have so many pictures of her.
● Talk about what is meant by a 'famous person'. Can the children suggest people that are famous today?
● Explain to the class where Florence Nightingale was born and look at the map or globe together, to locate Italy and Florence.
● Discuss the context of the pictures and ask what else they tell us about her work, such as the kind of hospitals that she worked in.
● Give the children drawing, sketching or painting materials and set them the task of making their own portraits of Florence.

Plenary

● After collecting in the children's work, look at a selection of the completed portraits with the class and evaluate them in terms of what they show about Florence Nightingale.

Differentiation

Direct your questions carefully and match them to the abilities of different children in the class.

Links
NC English KS1: En1 (1) to speak clearly and with confidence; (2) to listen and respond to others.
NC Geography KS1: (2a) to use geographical vocabulary; (2c) to use globes and maps.
NC Art and design KS1: (2c) to represent observations and make images.

The story of Florence Nightingale

Objectives
● To find out about the past from written sources.
● To communicate their knowledge of history in a variety of ways.

Vocabulary
hospital, ward, lady, lamp

Resources
Enlarged copy of the photocopiable sheet 'The story of Florence Nightingale' on page 98; wordbank or children's wordbooks.

Links
NLS Y1-2 Word level work: vocabulary extension by using words linked to a particular topic; Sentence level work: sentence construction; Text level work: non-fiction work, reading comprehension.
NLS Y1 T3 Text 19: to use text to find answers; Text 22: to record information from texts.
NLS Y2 T3 Text 16: to scan a text to find specific sections; Text 19: to make simple notes from non-fiction texts.

Background
Stories provide a rich source of information about the past in a form that is readily understandable to young children. This story can be used to inform children about the life of Florence Nightingale, to acquaint them with conditions in Victorian times and also to teach them simple skills in finding information from written sources.

Introduction
● Discuss how Florence Nightingale is considered to be a famous person because of the work she did.
● Explain that the children are now going to read a short story of Florence Nightingale's life and the things that she did.
● Display your enlarged version of the photocopiable sheet 'The story of Florence Nightingale' on page 98.

Main teaching activity
● Read the photocopiable sheet with the children. Explain that this is a story written about Florence Nightingale by someone who has read about her work.
● Ask questions such as: *Why was the story written? What can we find out from it about what Florence was like and about the kind of work she did?*
● Encourage the children to use the story to find information about Florence Nightingale, her work and what it was like to be in the Crimea at that time. Ask questions that require the children to look at the text to find the answer, for example: *What did Florence Nightingale buy for the soldiers?*
● Help the children to pick out key words from the text and to build up a collection of useful words in the class wordbank or in their individual wordbooks, for later use in the topic.

Plenary
● Challenge the children to read the key words that were chosen earlier. Work with the children to put the words into short, informative sentences about Florence Nightingale, based on what they have learned in the lesson. Display the words around the room or as part of a visual display about Florence Nightingale.

Differentiation
Differentiate questioning for different abilities: direct simple questions to less able children (for example: *Who is the story about?*) and more complex questions to more able children. Support less able children in picking out and reading key words from the text. Make sure that all the children in the class have understood the story.

What is being a nurse like?

Objectives
- To find out about the past from visual sources.
- To recognise similarities and differences between being a nurse today and a long time ago.

Vocabulary
drawing, photograph, old-fashioned, modern

Resources
Enlarged picture of Florence Nightingale; enlarged picture of a modern nurse; the photocopiable sheet 'What did Florence Nightingale use?' on page 99, one per child and one enlarged for whole-class work.

Background
Children can learn about the past by comparing features of past life with their modern equivalents. By looking at a modern nurse, children will more fully understand the role of Florence Nightingale, as well as begin to see how working as a nurse has changed over time.

Introduction
- Say to the children that they are going to look at a picture of Florence Nightingale, to see what she was like, how she dressed and the sort of equipment she used.
- Explain that they are then going to compare this with a picture of a modern nurse, who works in a hospital today.

Main teaching activity
- Look at the two enlarged pictures with the class.
- Ask general questions to encourage historical enquiry, such as: *What sort of picture is this – a drawing or a photograph? What can we find out from the pictures? What is different about the way Florence Nightingale dressed and what the modern nurse is wearing? What sort of equipment do nurses have now? What did Florence Nightingale have? Why are these pictures especially useful?*
- As a shared writing activity, make a chart on the board, or on an overhead projector, using the headings 'Same' and 'Different'. Write down the children's responses under the appropriate headings.
- Display your enlarged copy of the photocopiable sheet 'What did Florence Nightingale use?' on page 99 and give the children a copy each.
- Talk about the objects with the children, explaining what they are. Make sure that all the children understand that some of the objects are old and that some are modern. Complete one example together as a whole class and let the children finish the activity individually.

Plenary
- Go through the photocopiable sheet and check the children's answers together. Ask volunteers to say why they think certain objects would have been used by Florence Nightingale and others would not have been.
- Ask the class to think about the equipment that was available to Florence Nightingale and use the pictures to ask them whether it was easy to be a nurse when Florence Nightingale began her work.

Differentiation
Younger or less able children may need support during the completion of the activity sheet. More able children could be encouraged to write extended sentences, comparing nurses in the 19th century with modern nurses.

Links
NLS Y1–2 Word level work: vocabulary extension by using words linked to a particular topic.
NLS Y2 T3 Text 21: to write non-chronological reports.

Where is the Crimea?

Objectives
- To understand why Florence Nightingale acted as she did.
- To locate the site of a historical event on a map or globe.

Vocabulary
map, globe, world, Crimea

Resources
The photocopiable sheet 'A route to the Crimea' on page 100, one per child and one enlarged for whole-class work; globe of the world; coloured pencils; thick cotton and pins.

Links
NC English KS1: En1 (1) to speak clearly and with confidence; (2) to listen and respond to others. NC Geography KS1: (2c) to use globes and maps.

Background
The Crimean War occurred between 1854 and 1856. Scutari was a British army base in a suburb of Constantinople (now Istanbul), and it was also the site of the military hospital where Florence Nightingale worked. This lesson is designed to help children understand where Scutari is and that there was a war going on there, which involved British soldiers. They can be helped to understand that it was because of this war that Florence Nightingale was asked to go to work as a nurse there. Florence Nightingale had a long journey to make. With a group of nurses that she had recruited, she set off across the English Channel. She then had to travel through France to the Mediterranean port of Marseilles, where she caught another ship which would take her to Scutari. This was a long and difficult journey in Victorian times.

Introduction
- Look at the globe of the world with the class and ask them to think about questions such as: *Where is the Crimea? Where did the Crimean War take place? Where is Scutari?*
- Help the children to find where Britain is on the globe, and then where the Crimea is.
- Discuss the distance it was to travel and talk about the kinds of travel available in those days – horses and carriages, sailing ships – all very slow.
- Prompt the children to think in further detail with questions such as: *How did Florence get to Scutari? Where do you think she stayed while she was travelling? What about when she got there?*

Main teaching activity
- Provide each of the children with a copy of the photocopiable sheet 'A route to the Crimea' on page 100, showing the main places on Florence Nightingale's journey.
- Look at the places on the map with the children and help them to find key points on it.
- Discuss why Florence went this way.
- Work with the children to trace her route and to colour the land and seas that she crossed.

Plenary
- Display the enlarged version of the map and pin Florence Nightingale's route on to it using thick cotton and pins.

Differentiation
Less able children will need help in identifying the land and sea areas on their maps. Encourage more able or older children to copy out the names of some of the places listed.

Listening to Florence Nightingale speak

Objectives
● To find out about the past from oral sources.

Vocabulary
speak, record, sound

Resources
Recording of Florence Nightingale speaking (for example, from the website for the 'Oral history' section of The British Library Sound Archive at: www.bl.uk/collections/ sound-archive/ history.html); the transcript enlarged for display.

Background
There is an early cylinder recording of Florence Nightingale speaking. She was 70 years old when it was made and the recording hisses and crackles, but it is still possible to make out what Florence Nightingale is saying. She speaks in a very different manner from today's everyday style of speech. The recording throws light upon her own view of her work. She certainly seems proud of her achievements.

Transcript of the recording:
'At Florence Nightingale's house, London, July the 30th, Eighteen hundred and ninety. When I am no longer even a memory, just a name, I hope my voice may perpetuate the great work of my life.'

Introduction
● Explain to the class that, as well as pictures and photographs, we have a recording of Florence Nightingale speaking. We can hear her voice and how she spoke.

Main teaching activity
● Listen to the recording of Florence Nightingale speaking and show the children an enlarged copy of the words she is saying.
● The class is likely to need to listen to the recording several times over, since it is not very clear or easy to make out what she is saying.
● Read through the transcript.
● Ask the children: *How do we know this is an old recording?* Talk about the sound of the recording and how we know it was made a long time ago.
● Invite the children to describe the way Florence Nightingale speaks. What does it tell us about her?
● Discuss how this way of talking seems very old-fashioned to us now.
● Ask the children to pick out words and phrases that they would not use when they are talking today.

Plenary
● Make a list with the class of the differences in the way Florence speaks, compared with modern-day speech.

Differentiation
Differentiate questions for the different abilities or age groups within the class. Ask less able children simple, direct questions, for example: *Who is this speaking?* For more able or older children, ask further questions, such as: *How long ago was this recording made?*

Links
NLS Y1–2 Word level work: vocabulary extension by using words linked to a particular topic.
NC English KS1: En1 (2a) to sustain concentration when listening.

Hot-seating

Objectives
● To find out about the past from role play and drama.

Vocabulary
question, dress up, role, character

Resources
Items of old-fashioned clothing, such as: a frilly cap, shawl, long skirt; toy jewellery; small lamp or candle and candlestick.

Background
Hot-seating is a good way of providing first-hand experience for the children. In this lesson you take on the role of Florence Nightingale and the children will have the opportunity to interview her. Children respond well to people in role and will be able to relate to the notion of Florence Nightingale as a real person, understanding her pride and commitment to her work as a nurse.

Introduction
● Explain the lesson objectives to the class: they are going to find out more about Florence Nightingale by asking her questions.
● Ask the children what they can remember about Florence Nightingale and her work. If necessary, spend some time reminding the children what they have learned previously.
● Prepare some questions with the children that they would like to ask Florence Nightingale if they had a chance to meet her. Prompt them by saying, for example: *How could we find out more about Florence Nightingale? What sort of things could we ask her?*
● With the children, write these questions on the board, or prepare them on a sheet, with space for writing under each question.

Main teaching activity
● Enter the classroom in role, wearing some items of clothing such as a shawl and perhaps carrying a small lamp or candle.
● You may decide to be Florence Nightingale once she has become quite old and, if this is the case, you could use a walking stick.
● Introduce yourself as Florence Nightingale, using the same tone and manner of speech as that heard in the recording in Lesson 5.
● Once seated, tell the children about your life history and then ask them if there is anything they want to ask you about. If the children are reticent about asking questions, encourage them by reminding them of the questions they thought of earlier.
● When the 'interview' is over, thank them for being polite and considerate listeners. Leave the room and return as teacher.

Plenary
● Once back in your role as teacher, ask the children, as an assessment activity, what they have found out from talking to Florence herself.

Differentiation
Less able children will need more support in asking a question, but try to make sure they participate fully in the activity. You could also organise the children to work in mixed-ability pairs or small groups to think of questions to ask Florence Nightingale, before compiling a complete list on the board or sheet together as a class.

Links
NLS Y1 T3 Text level 22: to write own questions; Y2 T3 Text level 19: to make simple notes.
NC English KS1: En1 (1) to speak clearly and with confidence; (2) to listen and respond to others.

Scenes from Florence Nightingale's life

Objectives
● To communicate historical knowledge through drama.

Vocabulary
journey, set sail, arrive, work, nurse

Resources
Simple story about the work of Florence Nightingale (such as the photocopiable sheet 'The story of Florence Nightingale' on page 98); pictures; cards to label significant scenes in her life.

Background
Children will gain a better understanding of who Florence Nightingale was and what she did by re-enacting key scenes from her life. Through role play the children can empathise with Florence Nightingale's situation and achieve a more direct learning experience. They will need to consider many factors, such as: the way people spoke in the 19th century, what Florence Nightingale was like, and how other people may have reacted to her.

Introduction
● Tell the children that they are going to learn about Florence Nightingale by using drama to re-create some scenes from her life.
● Divide the class into groups of between four and six children for the drama work, depending on the total number of children.

Main teaching activity
● Read the story of Florence Nightingale with the whole class.
● Ask the children to pick out four or five of the key events in the story, for example: Florence Nightingale hearing the news about her trip to the Crimea; setting sail; her horror at the situation she finds on arrival; her team of nurses working hard at Scutari to improve conditions; Florence arriving back at home.
● Assign an event to each group and explain that they will each re-enact a scene to tell the story of Florence Nightingale's life.
● Each group can create a large label on card, stating the focus of their scene, for example: 'setting sail'.
● Provide the children with pictures to use as a stimulus.
● Allow the children enough time to practise the scene. Depending on their ability, they could, for example, use role play or a freeze-frame to depict the scene.

Plenary
● Read the story again with the children acting out their scenes in sequence. Music and sound effects could be added if time allows. Rehearse the sequence and story over a few days for a presentation to parents, another class or the school in an assembly. For the class presentation, you could be the narrator or you could work on a script with one of the children to tell the story.

Links
NC English KS1: En1 (1) to speak clearly and with confidence; (2) to listen and respond to others; (4) to participate in a range of drama activities.

Differentiation
It will be useful to have groups of mixed abilities for this activity, as each child will be able to participate at their own level and will have something to offer to the role play. More able or older children may be able to work on a simple script of their scene.

The nurses' stories

Background
It is valuable for children to begin to understand that history is written in different ways by different people, depending on their personal point of view. Often a person, regarded as famous and important by one historian, may be cast as a villain by another. The use of these two passages will help children to begin to understand the complexities of the past. The style of language used in them will, however, be unfamiliar to the children, and could also be used as a teaching point.

Introduction
● Explain that the children are going to hear two nurses' accounts to give them an understanding of what it was like at Scutari from someone other than Florence Nightingale.

Main teaching activity
● Display the enlarged copy of the photocopiable sheet 'Two nurses' stories' on page 101. Read them through with the class.
● Ask the children what kind of accounts these are. Ask them questions, such as: *Why did the nurses tell their stories? Why are they especially useful to us now? What else do they tell us about Florence Nightingale and about life in the Crimean War for the nurses who worked with her?*
● Talk about the way the texts are written: it is easier to read them out loud because the nurses are writing as they would say these words.
● Use some shared-writing time to create a short story about life at Scutari written from the point of view of Florence Nightingale.
● Discuss with the class what she probably thought of the nurses, and how she felt about the hard work they were all doing there.
● Include some comments about the state of the hospital when they arrived and about what she tried to do.
● Decide whether Florence Nightingale is happy with her work or not. What about the two nurses?

Plenary
● Read through both versions of what it was like at Scutari, the point of view of Florence and then of her nurses, and discuss with the children how these stories are from different people and how they give different points of view. Compare this idea with disagreements that the children might have had about an incident.

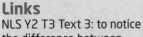

Differentiation
Younger or less able children will need additional support in understanding the language used in the extracts. Encourage more able children to write a few sentences of their own story.

A hospital play area

Objectives
● To communicate their learning about hospitals and nursing through role play.
● To apply their knowledge and understanding of hospitals and nursing a long time ago.

Vocabulary
hospital, patient, wounds

Resources
Small bed made from benches or boxes; props in the form of dressing-up clothes (such as: mop caps, long dresses, aprons and shawls), bandages, sheets, bowls, small cloths.

Links
NC English KS1: En1 (1) to speak clearly and with confidence; (2) to listen and respond to others; (4) to participate in a range of drama activities.

Background
Young children often learn best when they are actively involved in their learning. Structured play can allow them to use the knowledge they have gained to re-enact what they know. This activity also provides a useful assessment opportunity – you can observe and listen to see, from the way they act and talk, if the children have understood the timescale involved and the difference in conditions in the past and the present day. Because of the space needed for this activity, it will be easiest to use a large room or hall.

Introduction
● After setting out the required large items of furniture in the structured play area, such as the bed, explain to the class that the play area is going to be a ward in the hospital at Scutari.

Main teaching activity
● Ask the children what they would expect to see in this hospital ward a long time ago, for example: candles, a sheet for the bed, a blanket, bandages, walking sticks, and cleaning things for the nurses.
● Work with one group at a time in the play area, explaining how the boys would have been the wounded soldiers coming in as patients, while the girls would have had the job of the nurses. Some boys could be doctors or officers coming to see how the hospital is getting on.
● Help the children in the group to choose the characters that they want to be, to put on their costumes and to get into their roles.
● Allow them time to arrange all their 'equipment' and then to begin their role play of nursing the wounded.
● The groups can then take their turns at intervals over the course of the topic.
● As the role play progresses, observe the children to see how well they are making use of appropriate vocabulary and how well they have grasped the concepts of time and change. Do they have a good understanding of the situation in the hospital in the 19th century?

Plenary
● Once one or two groups have played in the hospital area, ask them what other things they think they might need. Discuss how hard it must have been when there were very few medicines so long ago.

Differentiation
Mixed-ability groupings will provide support for the less able children during their role-play sessions. Encourage more able children to extend the role-play activity to incorporate different viewpoints.

Sequencing events in Florence Nightingale's life

Objectives
• To sequence the events in Florence Nightingale's life.

Vocabulary
sequence, young, middle age, older

Resources
Enlarged copy of the photocopiable sheet 'The story of Florence Nightingale' on page 98; pictures to illustrate various scenes from her life; sentences of key events from the story on separate cards (one set for each group); paper and drawing materials.

Links
NLS Y1 T2 Text 4: to retell stories, giving the main points in sequence; Text 14: to represent outlines of story plots.
NLS Y1 T3 Text 5: to retell stories, to give the main points in sequence and to pick out significant incidents; Text 13: to write about significant incidents from known stories.
NLS Y2 T1 Text 4: to understand time and sequential relationships in stories; Text 11: to use language of time to structure a sequence of events.

Background
Children find time and chronology one of the most difficult concepts to grasp. It is important, therefore, to provide them with as many varied opportunities to develop this understanding as is possible. This lesson makes use of a story, a familiar type of information for them, in order to show the children how and why events can be put into a sequence. There is no need at this stage in children's learning to concern them with dates and periods, except possibly in passing.

Introduction
• Share a very simple version of the story of Florence Nightingale life with the class, for example, using the photocopiable sheet 'The story of Florence Nightingale' on page 98.

Main teaching activity
• Arrange the children in small groups. Give each group a set of cards with the sentences on, arranged in the wrong order.
• Invite the children to read the sentences through, supporting them as necessary.
• Ask them what they notice about these sentences. Discuss how they are not in the right order, or sequence, here.
• Encourage the children to say why it is important to tell a story in the correct order.
• Work with the children to sequence the main events from the story.
• When the groups are satisfied with their sequences, help the children to check their sentences against the original text. Do they want to make any changes to the order they have made?
• Ask the children to work individually and to draw a story sequence, or a set of pictures, one for each sentence, to tell the story of Florence Nightingale's life. It may be useful to have on display a selection of pictures that illustrate key events.
• Give the children enough time to complete their pictures.

Plenary
• Review a selection of the picture sequences made by the children. Are the events shown in the correct order?
• Emphasise the importance of sequence. Check that all the children understand why the correct order in a story or an account of someone's life is necessary.

Differentiation
Less able children will need adult support in reading and sequencing the sentences. More able children could write their own sequenced story of Florence Nightingale's life as an extension activity.

What we know about Florence Nightingale

Objectives
● To recap what they have learned about Florence Nightingale.

Vocabulary
know, learned, grid

Resources
The photocopiable sheet 'What do we know about Florence Nightingale?' on page 102, one per child; red and blue pens.

Background
This lesson helps the children to consider what they have learned about Florence Nightingale and how they found out. It uses a simple method of encouraging them to review their own knowledge and understanding. As such, it can also be used as an assessment opportunity for the teacher.

Introduction
● Review the topic with the class, asking the children: *What have we learned about Florence Nightingale? What do we admire about her? Why do we still remember her?*

Main teaching activity
● Provide each of the children with a copy of the photocopiable sheet 'What do we know about Florence Nightingale?' on page 102. (Alternatively, you could create a similar grid in an ICT programme to use as an electronic chart.)
● Read through the headings with the children to ensure they understand how the grid is to be used. Encourage the children to think about how the headings apply to different periods in Florence Nightingale's life.
● Complete the first part of the grid with the whole class, modelling how to organise information in the boxes.
● Encourage the children to complete the rest of the grid by themselves. Provide support as necessary.
● Once the children have finished the activity, check the grids together.
● Ask the children if they have learned a lot of new information about Florence Nightingale. How much did they know at the start of the topic? How much do they know now?

Plenary
● Discuss with the class the main things that other children might want to know about Florence Nightingale. What are the most important facts about her life and work?
● Compile a list from the children's answers in preparation for a class assembly about Florence Nightingale.

Links
NLS: Y1-2 Text level work: writing composition.
NC ICT KS1: (1b) to enter and store information in a variety of forms.

Differentiation
Letting the children work in mixed-ability pairings could be a way of providing support for the less able children. Make sure, however, that all the children participate fully in the activity. Less able children will need support with writing their answers in the grids. Encourage more able children to write more fully about what they have learned.

Assembly on Florence Nightingale

Objectives
● To communicate their knowledge of history in a variety of ways.

Vocabulary
biography, pictures, stories, assembly

Resources
Pictures, paintings, stories, maps and charts completed by the class in the course of the topic.

Background
Communicating what they have found out from their work in history is a vital part of children's learning. Organisation and communication is a key feature of the 'Knowledge, skills and understanding' section of the National Curriculum for History at Key Stage 1. Presentations to small groups, their own class or another class are also useful ways of involving the children in a formal presentation of their work.

Introduction
● Ask the class what they have learned about Florence Nightingale, and what they can remember about her.
● Review the work they have done in their books, or displayed in the classroom.
● Tell the children that they are to be in charge of an assembly about Florence Nightingale.

Main teaching activity
● Involve the children in selecting the props for the assembly.
● Group the children to work on their presentations of different aspects of their work together, for example:
  ● a biography of Florence Nightingale's life
  ● pictures and paintings of Florence Nightingale's life
  ● a picture sequence of the events in her life
  ● pictures of the hospital where she and her nurses worked
  ● stories by those who knew her, such as soldiers and nurses
  ● two children to introduce the sound recording of Florence
  ● Nightingale speaking to conclude the presentation.
● The children with pictures can hold up their work and say a few words about it in turn. Those with stories can read them out to the audience.
● Organise the whole class in their groups and rehearse the whole assembly in the room where it is to take place – this will give the children confidence.
● Hold the assembly.

Plenary
● Following the assembly, invite visitors to come into the classroom to look at the work produced over the course of the topic.

Differentiation
Organise the presentations appropriately according to the different abilities within the class, for example, the more able children could read stories or poems, while the less able or younger children could show pictures they have made, saying a few words about them.

Links
NC English KS1: En1 (1) to speak clearly and with confidence; (2) to listen and respond to others. NC Art and design KS1: (3a) to review what they and others have done.

Who was Mary Seacole?

Objectives
● To find out about the past from pictures and photographs.

Vocabulary
portrait, Jamaica, officers, hotel

Resources
Portraits and pictures of Mary Seacole; globe or map of the world; lengths of paper folded into 'concertina books'; drawing materials.

Background
Mary Seacole was very famous during the period following the Crimean War. Indeed, during the 19th century, she was considered the greatest black woman. Surprisingly, her story was never recorded in history books and has only fairly recently come to light once more.

Mary Seacole was born in Kingston, Jamaica, in about 1805. She was always interested in caring for the sick. She was trained in herbal medicine and cared for sick British officers while living in Jamaica. When she heard of Florence Nightingale's expedition to the Crimea, Mary Seacole applied to join. She was turned down by the government, possibly because she was black. Undeterred, Mary set off by herself, using most of her own savings, and visited Florence Nightingale at Scutari. Hearing that help was more urgently needed at the front, Mary Seacole went to Balaclava near the front line at Sevastopol, and set up a hotel and shop, where she also cared for sick soldiers and officers, using her herbal remedies. She was very much loved and appreciated by them, and was invited by the veterans to a special commemorative event in London when the war was over.

Introduction
● Tell the children that they are going to find out about a famous person from long ago and that she is called Mary Seacole.
● Ask who has heard about her before. Prompt them with questions, such as: *Why is she so famous? What did she do? How do we know?*

Main teaching activity
● Show the class a selection of pictures of Mary Seacole.
● Ask the children if they can guess what she was like as a person from looking at the pictures.
● Discuss what is meant by a 'famous person'.
● Say where she was born and look at the map or globe to locate Jamaica.
● Tell the story of Mary Seacole's life.
● Provide the class with pre-folded 'concertina books' and ask the children to draw a picture sequence of the things she did.
● Display the books along with their work on Florence Nightingale.

Plenary
● Look at the completed picture sequences. Encourage the children to write about why Mary Seacole might not have been invited to join Florence Nightingale in her work.

Differentiation
The more able children will be able to write short captions or sentences to accompany their pictures. Less able children will need support in sequencing their pictures.

Links
NLS: Y1–2 Word level work: vocabulary extension by using words linked to a particular topic.
NC Art and design KS1: (2c) to represent observations and make images.

Mary Seacole's adventures

Objectives
● To find out about the past from written sources.
● To communicate their knowledge of history in a variety of ways.

Vocabulary
British, hotel, store, front line, autobiography

Resources
Copy of the photocopiable sheet 'Mary Seacole's British Hotel' on page 103, enlarged for display; wordbank or children's wordbooks.

Links
NLS Y1 T3 Text 19: to use text to find answers; Text 22: to record information from texts.
NLS Y2 T3: Text 16: to scan a text to find specific sections; Text 19: to make simple notes from non-fiction texts.

Background
When Mary Seacole arrived in the Crimea, she believed she could be of more help to the soldiers if she were nearer to the fighting. She travelled to Balaclava and found a site nearby where she could begin to build what she called the 'British Hotel'. It began as a general store, where the soldiers could buy provisions. Soon it became a meeting and lodging place, and also a place where soldiers could find treatment for their illnesses. Mary Seacole would also ride out on her horse to treat wounded men at the front line. She later wrote an autobiography describing her experiences, called *The Wonderful Adventures of Mrs Seacole in Many Lands*. The non-fiction text on the photocopiable page is an extract from her book.

Introduction
● Explain to the class how Mary Seacole decided to go to the front line to help wounded soldiers.
● Discuss the meaning of 'the front line'.

Main teaching activity
● Talk about how Mary Seacole wrote a book about her experiences when she returned to London after the war. Explain that her book is an autobiography, and discuss what this means.
● Say that the piece of writing they are going to read is taken from her autobiography. It describes the place she established to help the soldiers, which was known as the 'British Hotel'.
● Read out loud the extract on the photocopiable sheet on page 103 and point out that this was written by Mary Seacole herself.
● Ask the children why they think Mary Seacole wrote the book. What does it tell us about the British Hotel?
● Discuss the way it is written in an old-fashioned style and encourage the children to give examples of this.
● Ask the children which words they have never heard before and explain their meanings.
● Help the children to select key words from the text and to build up a collection of useful words in the class wordbank or in their individual wordbooks.

Plenary
● Challenge the children to read their list of words. Work with the children to put the words into short sentences about Mary Seacole's British Hotel.

Differentiation
Differentiate the questioning for different abilities. Less able children will need more support in reading out words. Challenge older or more able children with more difficult words.

The story of Florence Nightingale

Florence Nightingale was born nearly two hundred years ago. She is often called 'The lady with the lamp'. She was born in 1820 in the town of Florence in Italy. She was called Florence because her parents named her after the place where she was born. Florence had a happy childhood and always loved caring for animals. As she grew older, she began to believe that God wanted her to help poor people, especially if they were ill. She began to study and work as a nurse.

After several years, Florence was asked to take a team of nurses to look after the soldiers wounded in a war that was going on far away. She set off in 1854, with a party of 38 nurses, to travel to the Crimea and to work in the military hospitals there. The main military hospital was at Scutari, and this is where Florence first arrived in November. She was upset at what she saw. There was no water, and no proper beds or wards, just long, dirty halls. The wind whistled down the corridors, rats ran everywhere and the rain ran in through the leaking roof. The doctors and officials did not like Florence and her nurses at first. They disapproved of women working as nurses in army hospitals.

Things grew worse, and soon the officials realised that Florence knew what to do and could help them. Finally, they asked for her advice and she was able to start her work. Florence and her nurses scrubbed the floors, made beds for the soldiers, and went shopping to buy food, clothing and medical equipment. She also bought pillows, mattresses and blankets for the soldiers' beds. When soldiers arrived at the hospital, they would be greeted by Florence. She made sure they had baths, clean clothes, had their wounds dressed and received some food. At night, Florence went round all the wards with her lamp to check that everyone was safe and comfortable. This is why she came to be called 'The lady with the lamp'.

In 1856 the war came to an end and Florence took a boat back to England. She was very weak because she had been ill herself and she could hardly stand up by the time she returned home. Eventually she regained her strength and went back to her work. In 1860 she set up the Nightingale Training School for nurses. For many years, until her death, Florence helped to run the school. Queen Victoria was so interested in her work that she invited her to Balmoral Castle and helped Florence with her work. Many people still regard her as the founder of modern nursing.

What did Florence Nightingale use?

◼ Match the objects with Florence Nightingale by drawing a line.

◼ When you have matched the objects from the past with the picture of Florence, colour in the old-fashioned ones that she would have used.

A route to the Crimea

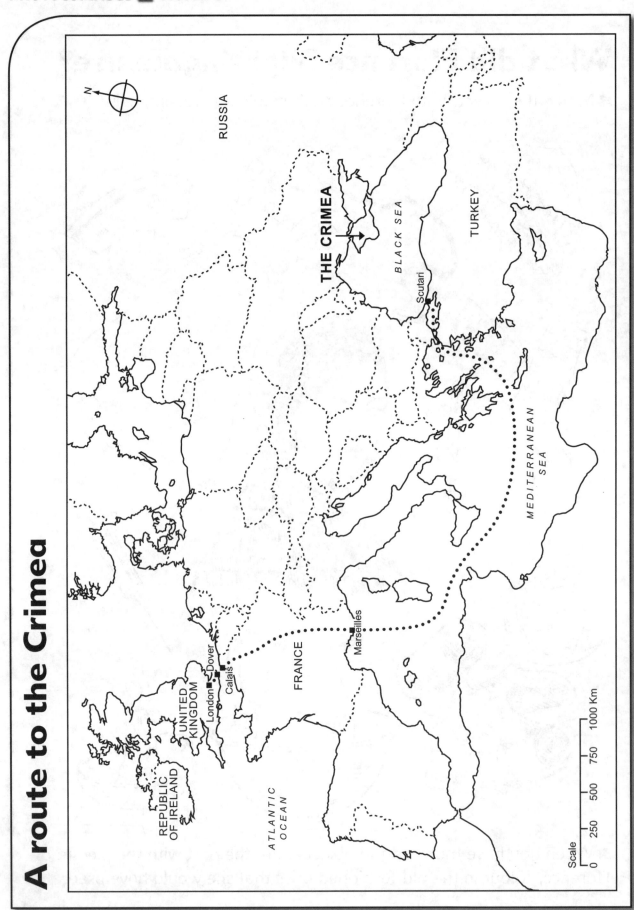

Two nurses' stories

Accounts by two nurses, telling what it was like to work for Florence Nightingale.

At Scutariar Baricks we are treated With the greates disrespect and unkindness by Miss nightingale and her housekeeper. She all but starves us an it is very hurtfull to our feelings. She picks out the wirst sortes of meate and We cannot get our teeth through and Magets get out on our plats.
(An anonymous St John's nurse)

Wee are all so very unappey Miss Nightingale have sum spite against us but for wat cawse wee know not. And Mrs Basebridge has treated us with Contempt ever since the day Mr Sheperd left us. I woold not minde wat harde ships wee had to incaunenter with if they woold be kinde to us. Thay treate us worse than the Coman low wimon they brate oute. I was never so unappey in My life, and wee are truley surrey that we ever came oute wothoute some one to care for us. We do the thing that is rite and if god be for us wee nead not feare. Mrs Clarke the housekeeper is a complete tirant she insults us every time she sees us Maryann in particular.
(Complaint by Mary Ann Coyle, another St John's nurse)

Extracts from *Tell Tale 4: Victorian Britain* by John West

What do we know about Florence Nightingale?

Fill in these boxes with what you have found out about Florence Nightingale.

Where did she live in different times of her life?

What was she like?

What did she do?

Where did she work?

Who worked with her?

SCHOLASTIC

Mary Seacole's 'British Hotel'

Let me, in a few words, describe the British Hotel. It was acknowledged by all to be the most complete thing there... The hotel and storehouse consisted of a long iron room with counters, closets and shelves, above it was another low room, used by us for storing our goods and above this floated a large Union Jack. Attached to this building was a little kitchen, ... – all stoves and shelves. In addition to the iron house were two wooden houses, with sleeping apartments for myself and Mr Day, outhouses for our servants, a canteen for the soldiery and a large enclosed yard for our stock, full of stables, low huts and sties. Everything, although rough and unpolished, was comfortable and warm and there was a completeness about the whole which won general admiration. The reader may judge of the manner in which we had stocked the interior of our store from the remark, often repeated by the officers, that you might get everything at Mother Seacole's, from an anchor down to a needle.

From *The Wonderful Adventures of Mrs Seacole in Many Lands* by Mary Seacole

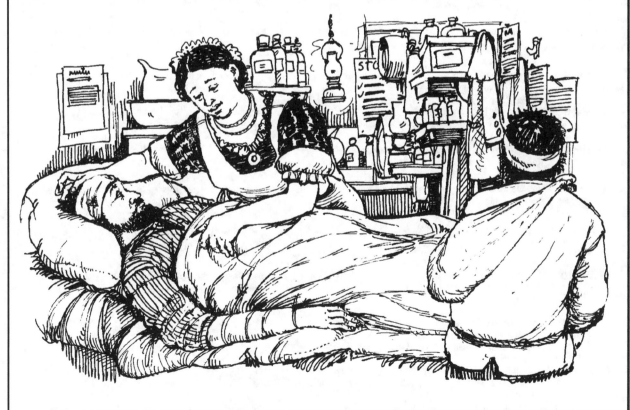

CHAPTER 6

Isambard Kingdom Brunel

This chapter supports the QCA Adapted Unit 'Why do we remember Brunel?' and looks at Isambard Kingdom Brunel's main activities and his contribution to society. Brunel's work as an engineer encompassed many dimensions, such as tunnels, railways, bridges, docks and ships. It is important to plan lessons according to the children's prior knowledge. For example, some children will be unfamiliar with steam engines and even trains. There is plenty of potential for cross-curricular activities, such as working with maps, because it is important for children to be aware of the places where Brunel worked. Looking at Brunel's bridges leads neatly into design and technology, while speaking and listening skills are always encouraged when talking about Brunel.

	OBJECTIVES	MAIN ACTIVITY
Lesson 1 P	To find out about Brunel using photographic information. To recognise that Brunel lived a long time ago and was a famous engineer.	Children look at a picture of Brunel and consider what it shows about him, working both as a class and individually using the photocopiable sheet.
Lesson 2 P	To find out about the building of the Great Western Railway, using a range of sources. To recognise Brunel's important contribution to the GWR. To know about the problems of railway building.	Looking at visual sources, children learn how the Great Western Railway was built. They then fill in a word grid and draw a picture of a train.
Lesson 3 P	To find out about railways in the time of Brunel. To identify similarities and differences between modern railways and railways in the time of Brunel.	Looking at pictures of a modern train and one from the 1840s, children identify key features and record similarities and differences.
Lesson 4	To find out about the ways in which railways affected people's lives. To show how the past is represented in different ways.	Children discuss the benefits of the advent of the railway, using video, pictures and a poem, and display their findings as a poster.
Lesson 5	To find out about the importance of the SS *Great Western*. To convey its importance, using an advertisement.	Children learn about the importance of the *Great Western* steamship and produce an advertisement.
Lesson 6	To find out about the SS *Great Britain* through research. To recognise why the SS *Great Britain* is an important ship.	Children access information about the SS *Great Britain* using a website and answer questions on a quiz sheet.
Lesson 7	To develop knowledge of Brunel's work as an engineer. To ask questions about Brunel's life.	An adult role plays Brunel so that the children can ask 'him' questions.
Lesson 8 P	To understand what happened on the *Great Eastern's* first voyage. To show that Brunel faced failures as well as successes.	Children create the front page of a newspaper, describing the explosion on the *Great Eastern*.
Lesson 9 P	To know and understand some key words associated with Brunel's life.	Children compile their own dictionary of Brunel words, using text and pictures to explain their meaning.
Lesson 10	To know about Brunel's work in building the Royal Albert Bridge. To design and make a simple model bridge. To test and evaluate their bridges.	A photograph of the Royal Albert Bridge is the starting point for the children to make their own bridges from craft materials.
Lesson 11 P	To chronologically sequence key aspects of Brunel's work. To reflect upon Brunel's life and to recognise his importance. To be aware of how Brunel's work affected people's lives.	Children create a timeline and then work individually, sequencing pictures of Brunel's achievements and completing a spider diagram.
Lesson 12	To find out about Brunel's achievements as an engineer. To communicate an understanding of Brunel's life and work through art and craft activities.	In groups, children create artwork showing aspects of Brunel's achievements for a large timeline collage.

A portrait of Brunel

Objectives
● To find out about Brunel using photographic information.
● To recognise that Brunel lived a long time ago and was a famous engineer.

Vocabulary
significant, important, famous, engineer, Brunel, waistcoat, top hat

Resources
The photocopiable sheet 'A picture of Brunel' on page 117, one per child and one copy of the picture enlarged for whole-class work; photographs of contemporary famous people with different achievements (for example, in sport); a simple timeline using string, pegs and date cards.

Links
NLS: Y1-2 Word level work: vocabulary extension by using words linked to a particular topic.

Background
A portrait is an effective introduction to a topic on a famous person: it allows children to quickly form an impression of the person and to relate to them. Aspects such as clothing, background and character can be observed and interpreted. Isambard Kingdom Brunel was born in Portsmouth in 1806, the son of a notable civil engineer. Brunel was involved in a range of ambitious projects that included railways, bridges and ships. The Great Western Railway founded his reputation as a great engineer. Unfortunately, Brunel died in 1859 amidst serious difficulties with the immense *Great Eastern* steamship.

Introduction
● Show a few photographs of famous people and ask if the children can name them.
● Introduce and discuss terms such as 'important' and 'famous'. Explain how these people have made significant contributions to different parts of life.
● Ask the children if they know of any famous people from the past. Tell the children that they will be finding out about an important person who lived a long time ago called Isambard Kingdom Brunel. Explain that most people call him by his surname - Brunel.

Main teaching activity
● Show the enlarged photograph of Brunel and ask the children what it tells us about him.
● What sort of clothes is he wearing? Encourage the children to refer to the top hat, waistcoat and winged collar. Do Brunel's clothes look familiar? Emphasise that his clothes are very different from today, showing that he lived a long time ago.
● Focus on the background and point out the chains. What might they be used for? What sort of job do the children think Brunel had?
● Explain that Brunel was an engineer who was famous for building ships, railways and bridges a long time ago.
● Give out the photocopiable sheet 'A picture of Brunel' on page 117 and work with the children to complete the activities.

Plenary
● Discuss the children's answers, reinforcing the idea that Brunel was a famous engineer. Conclude by using a simple timeline to show when Brunel lived - in the first half of the 19th century.

Differentiation
The more able children should be encouraged to explore Brunel's feelings and to explain the sort of work he did, using the supporting evidence. The less able children may need to bullet point their written answers.

The Great Western Railway

Objectives
- To find out about the building of the Great Western Railway, using a range of sources.
- To recognise Brunel's important contribution to the GWR.
- To know about the problems of railway building.

Vocabulary
Great Western Railway, Bristol, London, Paddington, navvy, tunnel

Resources
Portrait of Brunel (see Lesson 1 on page 105); railway pictures or videos; map showing the line from London to Bristol; pictures of key features, such as Box Tunnel and Paddington Station; the photocopiable sheet 'The Great Western Railway' on page 118, one per child; pictures and word cards relating to the railway; key points about the making of the railway written on transparencies; drawing materials.

Links
NC Geography KS1: (2c) to use maps and plans at a range of scales.

Background

Brunel was the chief engineer of the Great Western Railway, which connected Bristol in West England with London. Building began in 1835. Thousands of navvies ('navigator' was another name for manual workers) worked by hand. Brunel built the railway as straight and level as possible, but this required deep cuttings, embankments and viaducts. A large bridge was built across the River Thames at Maidenhead while, at Box near Bath, navvies cut a tunnel through two miles of rock (by candlelight, using gunpowder to blast the rock!) which took years to finish. The railway opened on 30 June 1841. A new steam engine, called *Fire Fly*, was specially built for this line.

Introduction

- Using the portrait of Brunel, tell the children that Brunel was famous for building railway lines.
- Ask the class to explain what a railway is and to talk about any train journeys they have made. Use pictures or video material to ensure that they understand what a railway looks like.
- Tell the children that in the lesson they will be finding out about how Brunel built a famous railway from London to Bristol.

Main teaching activity

- Using a storytelling style and pictures, explain how the Great Western Railway was built. Emphasise that Brunel designed it and was in charge of its construction. Support the story with appropriate pictures, word cards and key points summarised on transparencies.
- Show Bristol and London on a map. Explain that the railway that joined them was called the Great Western because it linked London with Bristol in the west.
- Explain that navvies did the actual manual work, often only using picks, shovels and wheelbarrows.
- Highlight some of the problems faced by Brunel and the need to build bridges, cuttings, embankments and a tunnel.
- Ask the children to complete the word and drawing activities on the photocopiable sheet 'The Great Western Railway' on page 118.

Plenary

- Ask the children for the answers to the word grid and talk about the words.
- Reinforce key points about building the Great Western Railway, including problems faced and achievements like Box Tunnel.

Differentiation

The strong focus on visual material should provide learning opportunities for all abilities. The word grid can be adapted to make it more or less difficult to cater for the ability range.

Railways now and then

Objectives
● To find out about railways in the time of Brunel.
● To identify similarities and differences between modern railways and railways in the time of Brunel.

Vocabulary
steam engine, carriages, electric train, similar, different

Resources
Pictures of railways today and in the time of Brunel; flipchart paper and pens; the Great Western Society website for information about the *Fire Fly* steam locomotive and pictures (www.didcotrailwaycentre. org.uk); the photocopiable sheet 'Railways then and now' on page 119.

Links
NC Art and design KS1: (4c) differences and similarities in the work of artists, craftspeople and designers in different times.

Background
An important aspect of KS1 History is allowing children to compare present with past and to identify changes which have taken place. For the modern era, a picture of Virgin's new high-speed Pendolino train would be ideal. Good visual material can be sourced from readily available railway videos, magazines and websites. For the 1840s period, the Great Western Society website is useful. At the Society's base at Didcot in Oxfordshire, a replica working steam locomotive dating from the 1840s called *Fire Fly* was completed in 2005.

Introduction
● Show the children a picture of a Great Western Railway train of the 1840s. What can they see in the picture? Can they remember the name of the person who built this railway?
● Then show the children a picture of a modern railway scene and ask them for their observations. Encourage the children to talk about these pictures in terms of being old and modern.
● Explain that they will be finding out more about trains in Brunel's time and comparing them with the trains we use today.

Main teaching activity
● Look in more detail at trains from the present and the 1840s. What is similar? What is different? Access the Great Western Society's website to look at *Fire Fly* in action.
● Split the class into groups, giving each group a picture of a GWR train in the 1840s. Ask the groups to identify and record things in the picture, such as the steam engine, signals and the carriages.
● Give each group a picture of a modern-day railway scene with an electric or diesel train. Again, ask the children to identify key features.
● Revise what is meant by the words 'same' and 'different'. Looking at both pictures, groups can list similarities and differences.
● Bring the class together for the groups to share their ideas. Then highlight some key similarities and differences.
● Distribute the photocopiable sheet 'Railways then and now' on page 119, on which the children can record similarities and differences both in written and pictorial forms.

Plenary
● Ask for volunteers to say what similarities and differences they have identified. Which design of train do they like the most and why?

Differentiation
The less able children may need further clarification about what are similarities and differences. The more able children could use short sentences instead of bullet points. Extension work could focus on discussing and writing about which design they prefer and why.

The effects of railways

Objectives
- To find out about the ways in which railways affected people's lives.
- To show how the past is represented in different ways.

Vocabulary
goods, passengers, navvies, coal, seaside, mail, newspapers, animals, carriages

Resources
Picture of Brunel's Great Western Railway; map of the British railway system (a number of maps can be viewed on the National Rail website at www.nationalrail.co.uk/tocs_maps/); video and pictures of railways a long time ago; collection of pictures showing different uses and aspects of railways (such as carrying goods, a postal train, passengers, people working on or operating the railway); artefacts to demonstrate railways and their cargo (such as a model train set, bricks, coal or newspapers); poem 'From a Railway Carriage' by Robert Louis Stevenson; flipchart paper and pens.

Links
NC English KS1: En2 (6f) to use poems that are challenging in terms of length or vocabulary.

Background
The 'railway mania' of the 1840s led to the rapid building of lines throughout the United Kingdom. The country was transformed with steam trains transporting passengers and goods faster and more cheaply than roads or canals. It is important that children develop some awareness of these improvements. Use photographs to highlight some of the following results of the railway: jobs building or running the railway, passenger travel (such as trips to the seaside), the carriage of newspaper and mail, the transport of many different types of goods, such as coal, bricks, wood, iron, animals and food.

Introduction
- Show the children a picture of Brunel's Great Western Railway and ask them to recall some key facts about the GWR.
- Emphasise that in the 1840s the railway was a new type of transport that linked many towns and villages. A map of the railway system will illustrate the major places that are linked by railway.
- Explain to the class that the building of railways had a big effect on people's lives.

Main teaching activity
- Show and discuss a video or some pictures of railways a long time ago that highlight some of the benefits of railways, like carrying passengers quickly and transporting a wide range of goods.
- Read 'From a Railway Carriage' by Robert Louis Stevenson and discuss how it emphasises the speed of travelling by train.
- Split the class into groups and give them a set of railway photographs that show the different results of the advent of railways.
- Ask the children to use the pictures to find out how people benefited from railways. Artefacts, like a piece of coal, a brick or a newspaper, could be used to emphasise what the railways carried. Carriages and wagons from a model railway set would also be useful.
- Ask groups to produce a poster with key words and pictures summarising some of the benefits and uses of railways.

Plenary
- Ask the groups to report back their findings. Ensure that the children are aware of how railways provided transport for passengers and goods as well as creating jobs. Conclude by explaining that, although railways made many people's lives better, there could be unpleasant results, such as smoke and pollution from steam engines.

Differentiation
Children working in mixed-ability groups should all be able to contribute to the poster. Monitor groups carefully and encourage everyone to participate in both the poster activity and the plenary.

The SS *Great Western*

Objectives
● To find out about the importance of the SS *Great Western*.
● To convey its importance, using an advertisement.

Vocabulary
steamship, paddle wheels, Bristol, New York, funnel, sails, Atlantic Ocean, passengers, cargo

Resources
Picture of New York; advertisement for flights to the USA; picture of the *Great Western* steamship; map showing North America, England and the Atlantic Ocean; advertisement for a modern ocean liner such as the *Queen Mary 2*; advertisement frameworks for children.

Links
NC Geography KS1: (3b) to identify and describe where places are on a map.
NC Science KS1: Sc4 (2a) to find out about and describe the movement of familiar things.
NC Design and technology (4b): how mechanisms can be used in different ways.

Background
Brunel also became famous for developing ocean-going steamships. With many people wanting to leave England to start a new life in America, Brunel argued that Bristol should develop as a departure point for passengers. In 1836 construction began on Brunel's SS (steamship) *Great Western*. She was built of wood and was fitted with paddle wheels powered by steam engines. The *Great Western* left Bristol on 8 April 1838 bound for New York, arriving just 15 days later. Over the next eight years the *Great Western* provided a regular service to New York. A reliable and safe vessel, the *Great Western* offered the first successful and regular transatlantic service.

Introduction
● Show a picture of modern New York and encourage the children to recognise it as an important place that is far away in the United States of America.
● Talk about how we travel to America today.
● Show an advertisement for an airline flying to America. Ask the children what an advertisement is and what features it has.
● Explain that in the time of Brunel the only way to travel to America was by sea, so Brunel built an important ship that started a regular service to New York.

Main teaching activity
● Introduce a picture of the SS *Great Western* and ask the children to identify parts of the ship, such as the sails, paddle wheels and funnel.
● Talk about why Brunel wanted to build a steamship to transport people between Bristol and New York.
● Show the locations of Bristol and New York on a map. Emphasise the long distance and the dangers of crossing a big ocean.
● Tell the children that they are to produce their own advertisement for the *Great Western*. Look at a modern example for ideas.
● Identify features and details that the children could include, such as pictures, the ship's name, the destination, sailing date and journey time. Ideas need to be clearly displayed for reference purposes.
● Give children a framework for their advertisement to help them with the structure and their writing.

Plenary
● Display the children's advertisements. Ask the children to explain why the *Great Western* was so important.

Differentiation
Use a variety of advertisement formats to cater for differing abilities. The less able children could focus on a picture and slogan, while others could produce more text.

The SS *Great Britain*: a quiz

Objectives
● To find out about the SS *Great Britain* through research.
● To recognise why the SS *Great Britain* is an important ship.

Vocabulary
Great Britain, internet, Bristol, preserved, iron, propeller, steamship, Australia

Resources
The SS *Great Britain* website at www.ssgreat britain.org; pictures of the *Great Western* and *Great Britain*; a quiz sheet with questions relating to information found on the SS *Great Britain* website or relevant reference books; word cards for each stage of the ship's life; computers, one per pair of children.

Links
NC ICT KS1: (1a) to gather information from a variety of sources.

Background
Brunel built a much larger iron-hulled ship called the SS *Great Britain* in 1843. At the time it was the largest ship in the world, using propellers instead of paddle wheels. Her first voyage was in 1845 to New York. Unfortunately, in 1846, the ship ran aground on the Irish coast. The salvage operation was expensive, and the *Great Britain* was sold after it was towed back to Liverpool in 1847. Under new owners the *Great Britain* made many successful voyages from Liverpool to Australia. Damaged off Cape Horn in 1866, the ship reached the Falkland Islands and was abandoned. The ship's historical significance resulted in her salvage and return to Bristol in 1970 for preservation.

Prepare a quiz sheet on the *Great Britain* with a variety of question styles, using both text and pictures, Use relevant reference books if an internet connection is not available.

Introduction
● Begin by talking about the *Great Western* steamship. Emphasise its success and how Brunel wanted to build a bigger and better ship.
● Talk about the history of Brunel's second ship, the *Great Britain*, and show an old and modern picture of the ship. Encourage the children to recognise that the ship has been preserved to show what it used to look like.
● Tell the class that they will be finding out more about the *Great Britain* for themselves.

Main teaching activity
● Display the *Great Britain* website and navigate through some of the sections. Show the children the different images of the ship, subheadings and text.
● Give the children a quiz sheet and ask them to work in pairs to find out some key facts about the *Great Britain* from the website or other resources provided.
● Monitor the pairs carefully as they work on the computers or use reference books.

Plenary
● Bring the class together and work through the answers to the quiz. Ensure they recognise that the *Great Britain* was important because she was the first propeller-driven ship to cross the Atlantic Ocean.
● Conclude by summarising the main stages in the ship's history, using word cards.

Differentiation
Working in pairs will promote mutual support. Work round the class to guide their searches and keep them focused on the quiz. Encourage the children to use the pictures to understand the text.

An interview with Brunel

Background
Children will benefit from role play and hot-seating for any Key Stage 1 topic that focuses on a significant individual. By talking to an adult taking the part of Brunel, the children can begin to see a real person who lived a real life. Although you could take on the role, bringing in an outside visitor is a good alternative. It is even better if the person can use authentic costume. Clearly, whoever plays Brunel will need to be very familiar with his work, and the session will need careful planning and structure. Recording the interview will allow the class to revisit what Brunel has said throughout the topic.

Introduction
● Explain to the children that they will be meeting Brunel, who will talk to them and answer any questions they might like to ask.
● Discuss together the sort of questions the children could ask. Write these up on the board and let the children make their own record, providing support as necessary.

Main teaching activity
● Introduce Brunel to the children and ask him to say something about his life and work. Use visual material during the talk to help the children understand more clearly what is being said.
● Allow the children to put their questions to Brunel. Some possible questions are: *What would you like to be remembered for? What work as an engineer did you like best? What problems did you face building the Great Western Railway? Can you tell us about the* Great Western *steamship? What successes have you had as an engineer? What failures have you had as an engineer? Was any of your work dangerous?*
● Ensure that any new vocabulary is put on the board and explained.
● Let the children choose three or four questions that they have asked Brunel. They can then record some answers in writing and pictures.

Plenary
● Discuss the answers that the children have recorded and encourage them to say what they found out by talking to Brunel. Give an opportunity for any further questions to be asked and for Brunel to make any final comments.

Differentiation
The level of vocabulary used can be an issue. Monitor closely and create opportunities to discuss any unfamiliar words. Questions to ask Brunel could be discussed in the previous lesson and a written copy given to the children. Encourage less confident members of the class to ask questions.

The *Great Eastern*

Objectives
● To understand what happened on the *Great Eastern's* first voyage.
● To show that Brunel faced failures as well as successes.

Vocabulary
Great Eastern, River Thames, London, explosion, scaffolding, difficulty, funnel, Weymouth, newspaper, headlines

Resources
Map to show the route of the *Great Eastern's* first voyage; picture of the *Great Eastern* under construction; the photocopiable sheet 'The story of the *Great Eastern*' on page 120, enlarged for display; examples of newspapers; front-page template of a newspaper, one per child or group; pens.

Links
NC English KS1: En2 (2a) to use the organisational features of non-fiction texts.
NC English KS1: En3 (1e) to vary their writing to suit the purpose and reader.
NLS Y1 T2 Text 18: to read non-fiction books; Y1 T3 Text 20: to write simple recounts; Y2 T3 Text 20: to write non-fiction texts.

Background
The building of Brunel's *Great Eastern* steamship began in 1852. At almost 700 feet long, this was the biggest ship in the world at the time. The ship was designed with both paddle wheels and a screw propeller. There were many problems building the ship and she was finally ready for sea trials in 1859. Brunel died soon afterwards. The *Great Eastern* was not a successful passenger ship, but was highly effective in laying the first transatlantic cable. The example of the *Great Eastern* shows that engineers like Brunel often faced real difficulties with their work and could experience failure.

Introduction
● Show a picture of the *Great Eastern* under construction.
● Look at the picture in detail. What possible dangers might the workers have faced building the ship?
● Explain that this ship was called the *Great Eastern*, which was the largest in the world in the 1850s, and Brunel faced many difficulties with this project.

Main teaching activity
● Using the photocopiable sheet on page 120, read and discuss the story of the *Great Eastern's* first voyage and the explosion.
● Use a map to show the vessel's route from London, where the explosion took place, and the location of Weymouth at which the *Great Eastern* docked.
● Use a large picture of the *Great Eastern* to show that the explosion took place around the first funnel.
● Tell the children that this was a very important event. Where would we read about this? Encourage the identification of newspapers.
● Explain that the children are to produce their own newspaper report about the *Great Eastern's* first voyage.
● Discuss the key features of a newspaper.
● Write suggestions for the story about the steamship on the board.
● Provide the children with a newspaper front-page template to write their report. This can be done in groups or individually.

Plenary
● Review progress made and ask for volunteers to show their newspaper reports and to read aloud what they have written.
● Conclude by emphasising that engineers like Brunel faced problems and failures as well as successes.

Differentiation
Adapt newspaper formats to cater for various ability levels. More able children could produce a picture and short report, while less able children might be confined to a picture and headlines.

Brunel words

Objectives
● To know and understand some key words associated with Brunel's life.

Vocabulary
tunnel, engineer, propeller, steamship, railway, station

Resources
Word cards; dictionary for young children with text and pictures; reference materials about Brunel, including pictures and books; the photocopiable sheet 'Words about Brunel' on page 121, one per child; scissors; paper (or workbooks); pens; copies of the alphabet.

Links
NC English KS1: En2 (7b) to use dictionaries.
NLS Y2 T2 Text 16: to use dictionaries and glossaries; Text 17: to understand that dictionaries and glossaries give definitions; Text 20: to make class dictionaries of special interest words.

Background
A study of Brunel will involve the use of unfamiliar vocabulary that needs to be explained and reinforced at every opportunity. Activities that involve children developing a wordbank, glossary or dictionary are clearly beneficial for both literacy and historical purposes. Although the word activity described here is for a single lesson, it could be organised as a continuous theme across the topic.

Introduction
● Using word cards, display examples of vocabulary linked to the Brunel topic. Encourage the children to read the words out loud. Can they explain what the words mean?
● Then let the children see a simple dictionary. Ask them what sort of book it is. Emphasise that it is called a dictionary.
● Invite the children to explain what a dictionary contains. Highlight features, such as it contains words in alphabetical order and their meanings. Ask the children why dictionaries are useful. Refer to the help dictionaries give us when spelling words and also that we can use them to check what words mean.
● Explain that the children will be making their own mini-dictionary about Brunel.

Main teaching activity
● Give out the photocopiable sheet 'Words about Brunel' on page 121 and ask the children to cut the words into strips as indicated.
● Working in pairs, the children can take it in turns to ask one another the meaning of a word as a short quiz activity.
● Bring the class together and ask for a few words to be explained.
● Show how words are listed in alphabetical order in a dictionary. Using an alphabet, work with the children to place their words in alphabetical order.
● Ask them to stick the words in the correct order in their books.
● Let the children then add a brief text or a picture symbol alongside each word to provide a simple meaning. Provide access to some reference books to help with the children's explanations.

Plenary
● Ask for a few children to show their work and to explain what the words tell us about Brunel.
● Conclude by revising the key features of a dictionary and discussing the value of it.

Differentiation
Provide support in cutting the strips out, as necessary. The more able children could be given extra words and asked to give meanings in text only. The less able children may need to use picture symbols.

The Royal Albert Bridge

Background

Brunel's work as a railway engineer involved the design of some notable bridges. One of the most famous is the Royal Albert Bridge, which spans the Tamar estuary near Plymouth. Following the completion of the Great Western Railway to Bristol in 1841, Brunel oversaw the extension of the line into Devon and Cornwall. In 1844 the railway reached Exeter and soon work started on building the line to Plymouth. At Saltash, near Plymouth, Brunel was faced by the challenge of crossing the River Tamar. Work on the bridge started in 1853, and its opening in 1859 completed Brunel's main line from London to Penzance.

Introduction

● Show the class the photograph of the Royal Albert Bridge.
● Explain that this is one of Brunel's most famous railway bridges and the children are going to find out more about it and try to make their own bridge.

Main teaching activity

● Use a map to show the route of the railway from London to Penzance. Look closely at the Plymouth area, using a local map, and identify the need to cross the River Tamar.
● Encourage the children to look at the map and photographs to identify the difficulties of building a bridge in this location.
● Using the photograph, ask the children to point out important features, such as the large tubes, the supporting chains, the pier in the middle, the two main spans and the bridge deck.
● Ask the children to suggest why the bridge is so strong. Draw a few sketches to show how the stone piers support the iron bridge deck, which is also strengthened by the huge iron tubes and metalwork.
● Split the class into groups and set them a bridge-making activity, using a range of materials, such as construction straws or cardboard.
● Ask the children to discuss and sketch out their plans for the bridge before starting to build it. Give careful guidance to the groups with their designs.
● Allow the groups to build their bridges. A competitive element could be introduced by explaining to the groups that their bridges will be tested with weights when completed.

Plenary

● Allow each group to present their model and to talk about the design. Discuss the merits of each one.

Differentiation

The bridge-making activity is ideal for mixed-ability grouping where different skills are required. Encourage all the children to participate.

The importance of Brunel

Objectives
● To chronologically sequence key aspects of Brunel's work.
● To reflect upon Brunel's life and to recognise his importance.
● To be aware of how Brunel's work affected people's lives.

Vocabulary
tunnel, engineer, propeller, steamship, station, Great Western Railway, Great Britain, Royal Albert Bridge

Resources
Materials for a Brunel timeline; dated picture cards for Brunel's projects; the photocopiable sheet 'The work of Brunel' on page 122, one per child; pens and paper (or workbooks).

Links
NC Mathematics KS1: Ma2 (2c) to read and write numbers.

Background
Towards the end of any unit, it is important to summarise the key points that have been covered and to allow the children to demonstrate what they have learned. At Key Stage 1 written assessment activities in history are valuable, but asking children to talk about Brunel's work and achievements will be equally useful. Self-assessment by the children should also be encouraged. What have they learned about Brunel? Have they enjoyed the topic? There is also scope in a session like this for setting a pictorial assessment of Brunel's achievements, with the children producing a special postage stamp or medal commemorating his work.

Introduction
● Explain that this session will focus on recalling Brunel's work and thinking about his importance.
● Revise the meaning of words like 'important', 'famous' and 'significant'. Emphasise that Brunel is important because his work as an engineer helped to change people's lives.
● Using pegs and string, construct a simple timeline covering Brunel's life from 1806 until his death in 1859.

Main teaching activity
● Ask the children to identify different examples of Brunel's work as an engineer, such as the Great Western Railway, the steamship *Great Britain* and the Royal Albert Bridge.
● Using a dated picture card for each of these, ask for volunteers to put them on the timeline in chronological order.
● Give out the photocopiable sheet 'The work of Brunel' on page 122. Ask the children to cut out the pictures of the key events, find the correct caption, sequence them chronologically and stick them in their books or on to paper.
● After they have completed this, ask the children to use the spider diagram to summarise why we remember Brunel.

Plenary
● Encourage the children to talk about the main events in Brunel's life and how his work affected people's lives. Ask some of the children to show their spider diagrams - are all the answers correct?
● Take time to review what has been covered during the topic and make sure that all the children have a good understanding of it.

Differentiation
Extra input might be needed with some children on chronological sequencing. For the less able children, the spider diagram might consist of a few bullet points. The more able children could be challenged to produce some detailed and higher level responses.

115

Creating a Brunel display

Objectives
● To find out about Brunel's achievements as an engineer.
● To communicate an understanding of Brunel's life and work through art and craft activities.

Vocabulary
Great Western Railway, the *Great Eastern* steamship, Clifton Bridge

Resources
Pictures and reference sources about Brunel, including websites, art and craft resources (such as paints, card, crêpe paper, glue, art straws, waste fabric materials); enlarged card-mounted pictures of Brunel's different projects (such as a GWR train, steamships and bridges); mannequin dressed in 19th-century style clothes (optional).

Links
NC Art and design KS1: (2a) to investigate the possibilities of a range of materials and processes; (2c) to design and make images and artefacts.

Background
A unit on an historic figure like Brunel provides an interesting range of opportunities for a classroom display which the children can help create. One idea is to produce a collage about his life that is structured into a timeline. Key features of his career can be included, such as the Great Western Railway (completed in 1841), the Clifton Suspension Bridge (completed after Brunel's death in 1864), the various steamships and the Royal Albert Bridge (completed in 1859). Outlines of these can be cut out in card with the children using various materials such as fabric, art straws and paint to add detail and colour. Another interesting idea is to re-create the famous portrait of Brunel in front of the *Great Eastern*'s launching chains. You could obtain a mannequin and dress it to represent Brunel.

Introduction
● Explain that the class will be helping to create a display about Brunel in the form of a collage.
● Ask for volunteers to suggest examples of Brunel's work that could be put into picture form in the collage. Write ideas on the board.
● Then introduce the large card cut-outs of subjects such as a GWR train, Clifton Bridge and the *Great Britain*. Can the children recognise what each portrays?

Main teaching activity
● Split the class into small groups, asking them to choose one of subjects, and give out the card cut-outs.
● Provide each group with a picture of their topic and encourage the children to look at it carefully.
● Show the children that they need to use the available resources to add detail, colour and texture to their card cut-outs. For example, string could be used to represent the vertical wires of the Clifton Suspension Bridge and a green material would be appropriate for the GWR steam engine.
● Monitor the group work carefully, encouraging the use of reference materials to inform the artwork.

Plenary
● Each group's picture will need to be assembled into the collage. Using captions and dates, involve the class in deciding where each picture should be positioned in the life of Brunel. The collage should be used actively with each group talking about their particular topic.

Differentiation
All groups will benefit from close support and the use of additional adults will really enhance this activity. Some children may need help with cutting out and safety issues are important.

A picture of Brunel

◾ Label objects in the picture, using the words in the box below.

| cigar | waistcoat | top hat | winged collar | watch chain |

◾ How do we know that Brunel lived a long time ago?

_____

_____

◾ What can you see behind Brunel? What material were they made from? What might they have been used for?

_____

_____

◾ What sort of job do you think Brunel had?

_____

_____

The Great Western Railway

◀ Fill in the missing letters using the clues below.

1. The railway crossed this famous river at Maidenhead.
2. A place where passengers get on the train.
3. At Box the train went underground through one of these.
4. A worker who helped build the railway was given this name.
5. The railway ran from London to this city.
6. The name of a steam engine on the Great Western Railway.

1 __T__ __ __ __ __ __m__ __ __ __ __ __ __

2 __ __ __t__ __ __ __ __ __ __ __o__ __ __

3 __ __ __n__ __ __ __l__ __

4 __N__ __a__ __ __ __ __ __ __ __

5 __ __r__ __ __ __ __o__ __ __

6 __F__ __ __ __ __ __ __ __ __ __ __y__

◀ Draw a picture of a train on the Great Western Railway.

Railways then and now

A train on the Great Western Railway in 1845

A train today

◣ Look at the pictures above and make a list of the things that are similar and the things that are different.

Similar	Different

The story of the *Great Eastern*

The building of Brunel's *Great Eastern* steamship began in 1852 on the River Thames near London. There were many problems with this huge iron ship, which was almost 700 feet long. It was not until September 1859 that the *Great Eastern* was ready to sail on her first trip, by which time Brunel was very ill and sadly not fit to travel on the ship.

When the *Great Eastern* first sailed, the weather was bad but she moved easily through the rough seas. As the ship passed Dungeness lighthouse, there was a loud explosion and clouds of steam shot up into the sky. People on deck saw the first of the ship's five tall funnels blown into the air. Broken wood, iron and glass lay everywhere. In the ship's boiler room six men who were putting coal on the fires died because of the escaping steam.

Despite this disaster the *Great Eastern* carried on without much delay and arrived at the port of Weymouth. It was later found that the explosion was caused by a mistake made by the builders. News of the terrible explosion on the *Great Eastern* quickly reached Brunel in London. He died in London soon afterwards at the age of 53 years.

The problems with the *Great Eastern* continued. The ship was not a success in carrying passengers, but it was used for laying cables under the sea. These cables allowed messages like telephone calls to be sent. The first telegraph message from America to England was the result of the *Great Eastern*'s work.

Words about Brunel

Word	What it means
Tunnel	
Train	
Engineer	
Steamship	
Railway station	
Famous	
Great Western	

The work of Brunel

◼ Cut out the pictures and match them with the correct captions at the bottom of this page.

◼ Put the pictures in the correct order of time and stick in your book.

◼ Copy this spider diagram into your book. Complete it to show why you think we should remember Brunel.

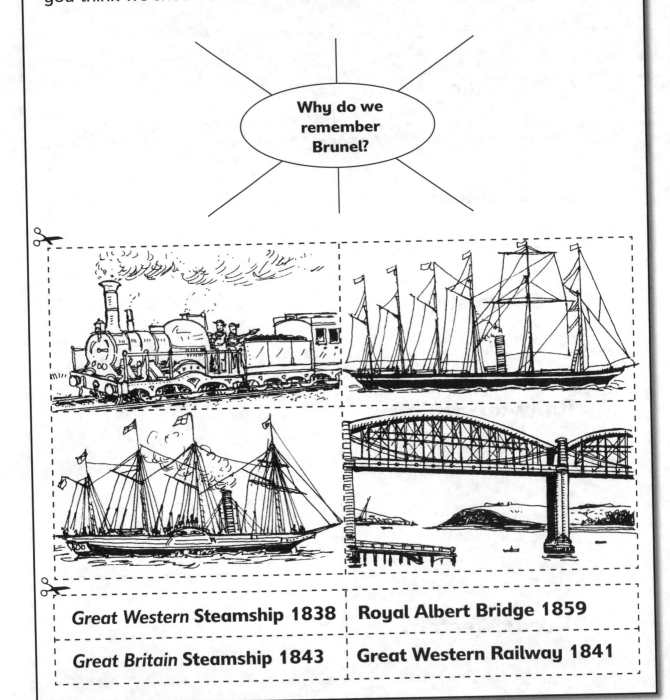

Why do we remember Brunel?

Great Western **Steamship 1838** | **Royal Albert Bridge 1859**

Great Britain **Steamship 1843** | **Great Western Railway 1841**

◼SCHOLASTIC

CHAPTER 7

The Great Fire of London

The Great Fire of London is one of the most popular KS1 History topics and the fascinating events so graphically brought to life by contemporary accounts, such as the diary of Samuel Pepys, provide interest for both children and teacher. The lesson plans in this chapter support the QCA History Unit 5: 'How do we know about the Great Fire of London?' The short duration of the fire allows a manageable timeline to be constructed, developing chronological understanding.

	OBJECTIVES	MAIN ACTIVITY
Lesson 1	To know that the Great Fire took place in London in 1666. To understand what London was like in 1666. To locate the Great Fire on a timeline.	Children look at modern London and a picture of London before the Great Fire. They investigate a portrait of Charles II.
Lesson 2 P	To understand where and how the fire started. To identify differences between baking then and now.	The story of the Great Fire leads the children to compare baking in the past and present and to make 17th-century cakes.
Lesson 3 P	To use a visual source to find out about the fire. To identify reasons why the fire spread so quickly. To understand that fire-fighting methods were very simple.	Children identify key features showing why the fire spread so quickly. Children label a picture of the fire.
Lesson 4	To find out about houses in London at the time of the Great Fire. To describe key features of houses at this time. To produce pictures and models of 17th-century houses.	In groups, children make a Great Fire frieze, researching and creating representations of 17th-century houses.
Lesson 5	To find out about Samuel Pepys by looking at a portrait. To understand that Pepys lived long ago. To know that he was famous for writing a diary. To understand the importance of eyewitness accounts.	Children investigate a portrait of Samuel Pepys. They draw their own pictures and write a few sentences, saying what Pepys was like.
Lesson 6 P	To find out about the Great Fire from Pepys' diary. To communicate their knowledge of the fire by making their own diary entries. To be aware of the importance of diaries as a genre.	Simplified extracts from Pepys' diary help the children to understand the Great Fire and this leads them to write their own diary entries.
Lesson 7	To identify differences between fire-fighting now and at the time of the Great Fire. To be aware of people like firefighters who help us in the community. To know about the importance of preventing fires.	Children learn about fire-fighting today and compare this with the past, by either going to a fire station or having a fire officer visit them.
Lesson 8 P	To use pictures and eyewitness accounts to find out about the different ways people escaped from the fire. To use drama to tell the story of how people escaped from the fire. To understand some of the feelings and emotions of people involved in the Great Fire.	Using pictures and accounts of the Great Fire, children consider how people must have felt. They then plan a role play to show how people escaped the fire.
Lesson 9 P	To place events of the fire in the correct chronological order. To introduce children to a timeline of the Great Fire. To know and be able to talk about the main events of the fire.	Together, children create a timeline of the Great Fire and then, using pictures on the photocopiable sheet, make one of their own.
Lesson 10	To know that the fire destroyed large parts of London. To understand how people were affected by the fire. To be aware that disasters still occur today.	In pairs, children produce a newspaper front page, describing the effects of the Great Fire on London and on its people.
Lesson 11	To know key words relating to the Great Fire. To develop an understanding of rhymes. To write a short poem about the Great Fire.	Children sing the rhyme 'London's Burning', create a list of associated words and write their own poem.
Lesson 12 P	To find out about the rebuilding of London. To understand the role of Sir Christopher Wren. To know about the building of St Paul's Cathedral and The Monument.	The work of Sir Christopher Wren is highlighted as children learn about the rebuilding of London and identify differences between the old and new city.
Lesson 13	To find out about the Great Fire by using a variety of sources. To ask and answer questions about the fire.	In groups, children research questions for a quiz. The whole class takes part in the quiz. Individually, children draw pictures.

What was London like at the time of the Great Fire?

100 HISTORY LESSONS: Ages 5-7

Objectives
● To know that the Great Fire took place in London in 1666.
● To understand what London was like in 1666.
● To locate the Great Fire on a timeline.

Vocabulary
London, River Thames, King Charles II, the Great Fire, the Stuarts, St Paul's Cathedral

Resources
Video or pictures of modern London; contemporary picture of the Great Fire; picture of London before the Great Fire (showing, for example, St Paul's Cathedral and the River Thames); map of the UK; portrait of King Charles II; timeline displaying the Roman period to the present (a different starting period could be used depending on the children's ability).

Links
NC Geography KS1: (3a) to identify and describe what places are like; (3b) to identify and describe where places are on a map.

Background
In the late 17th century London was the largest city in England with a population of about 450,000 people. The River Thames was busy with boats and the lifeline of the city, but only one bridge spanned it. Although some important buildings like churches were built of stone, many houses and other buildings were made of wood and packed closely together, which was a real fire hazard. King Charles II was king at this time, reigning from 1660 to 1685. His family name was Stuart and this name is given to this period of history.

Introduction
● Show a video or pictures of modern London with key landmarks. Ask the children if they know where these famous buildings can be found. Encourage them to identify the city of London.
● Show them where London is situated on a map of the UK. Compare this with the location of the children's school.
● Now show the picture of the Great Fire of London. What can the children see in the picture? Is this a new or an old picture? Do they know where the place is? Explain that the scene shows London a long time ago when there was a Great Fire.

Main teaching activity
● Display the picture of London before the Great Fire. Ask the children to look at it closely and to identify the different features.
● Ask the children to talk about the picture and list the different things they can see in it. Encourage them to notice how close together the buildings are and the materials they are made from. What might happen if a fire broke out?
● Working in pairs, ask the children to investigate the portrait of King Charles II. Encourage them to think about: what sort of picture it is; who is in the picture; the person's costume and hairstyle. Can they identify the person as a king? Do they know who a king is?

Plenary
● Ask the children to give feedback about the picture. Tell them that this is King Charles II, a very important person. Talk about why the period around the Great Fire is called the Stuart period.
● Locate 1666 on a timeline of English history. Discuss the term 'period' and encourage the children to view it as a block of time.

Differentiation
Questions about the portrait could be provided in a writing framework to help the children with written responses. By working in pairs, children can support one another and explore a greater range of ideas.

The start of the Great Fire

Objectives
- To understand where and how the fire started.
- To identify differences between baking then and now.

Vocabulary
wood, smoke, bakery, oven, roof, Pudding Lane, upstairs, Thomas Farynor

Resources
Painting of the Great Fire; map of London showing Pudding Lane; picture of Farynor's bakery; modern picture of baking; pictures of the fire starting and the escape of Farynor's family; the photocopiable sheet 'The start of the Great Fire' on page 137, one per child; recipe for 17th-century cakes (17th-century recipes can be found on the Gode Cookery website: www.godecookery.com/goderec/goderec.htm).

Links
NC Design and technology KS1: (2f) to follow safe procedures for food safety and hygiene.
NC Geography KS1: (3b) to identify and describe where places are on a map.
NLS Y1 T1 Text 13, Y2 T1 Text 13: to read and follow simple instructions.

Background
Before the widespread use of brick and stone, serious fires were commonplace because of the tightly packed wooden buildings. Traditionally the outbreak of the Great Fire is attributed to Thomas Farynor's bakery in Pudding Lane. One theory is that some wood in the bakery caught fire due to sparks from the oven. Starting in the early hours of Sunday 2 September 1666, a strong easterly wind helped the flames spread and by the morning over 300 houses had been destroyed.

To emphasise the role of the bakery in the fire, this lesson encourages the children to compare present-day baking with that in the17th century. You may wish to let the children make cakes from a genuine 17th-century recipe.

Introduction
- Show the picture of the Great Fire. Emphasise that this was a very big fire that destroyed a large part of London.
- Ask the children to suggest ways in which they think the fire could have started.
- Show a map of London highlighting Pudding Lane. Explain that the fire started here in a bakery.

Main teaching activity
- Tell the story of how the fire started in the baker's shop in Pudding Lane on 2 September 1666 and how it quickly spread out of control. Use pictures to illustrate the story including the family escaping.
- Look closely at a picture of Thomas Farynor's bakery. Discuss the differences between baking today and baking at the time of the fire.
- Use questioning to encourage the children to suggest what might have been made in this bakery at the time of the Great Fire, for example, bread and cakes.
- Introduce a recipe for cakes from the 17th century. Discuss the ingredients and instructions. Making some of these cakes would be an interesting extension activity(check for food allergies or dietary requirements first).
- Give out the photocopiable sheet on page137 and ask the children to work through the activities

Plenary
- Discuss the differences the children have found between baking now and at the time of the fire and start a wordbank.

Differentiation
The less able children could be given a word list for the labelling activity. Encourage more able children to write in full sentences when completing the photocopiable sheet.

The Great Fire spreads

Objectives
● To use a visual source to find out about the fire.
● To identify reasons why the fire spread so quickly.
● To understand that fire-fighting methods were very simple.

Vocabulary
street, bucket, spread, quickly, reason, straw, water squirt, strong winds

Resources
Large picture of a street scene during the Great Fire; the photocopiable sheet 'Why did the Great Fire spread so fast?' on page 139, one per child; picture of a water squirt.

Links
NC Geography KS1: (4a) to make observations about other features in the environment, for example, weather.
NC Science KS1: SC4 (2b) that both pushes and pulls are examples of forces.

Background
At Key Stage 1 children need to be encouraged not just to describe events like the Great Fire but also to explain in simple terms why they took place. They should be able to identify important reasons why the fire was so devastating, such as the wooden buildings and the strong wind. The lack of effective fire-fighting methods should also be a focus, including the use of water squirts. Tackling the fire was handicapped in the early stages by the hesitancy and inaction of the Lord Mayor, Sir Thomas Bludworth.

Introduction
● Show a large picture of a street scene with buildings ablaze and ask the children to recall how the fire started.
● Emphasise that the fire spread very quickly and that in the lesson they will be finding out why and identifying reasons. Discuss what is meant by the term 'reason'.

Main teaching activity
● Look at the picture in detail and encourage the children to identify features, such as the wooden houses with thatched roofs, narrow streets, churches, the flames out of control with people trying to stop the fire with buckets of water and water squirts.
● Can the children say why the fire spread so quickly? List reasons on the board, such as: the wooden buildings, narrow streets with overhanging houses, simple fire-fighting methods and no proper fire brigades.
● Tell the children that weather was also an important reason for the fire spreading. Can they say why? Emphasise how a hot summer made the buildings very dry and a strong wind helped the flames spread.
● Focus on the use of water squirts during the fire, using an enlarged picture to show what they were like. Do the children think water squirts would have been useful fighting the fire?
● Can the children suggest how a water squirt works? Parallels could be made with a water pistol.
● Give out the photocopiable sheet 'Why did the Great Fire spread so fast?' on page 138 and ask the children to label the scene.

Plenary
● Check the children's labelling and revise the main reasons for why the fire spread so quickly, highlighting key words on the board or using word cards.

Differentiation
Less able children will be helped by being provided with the labels for the picture. More able children could be challenged by encouraging extended writing, such as explaining how a water squirt worked.

Making a Great Fire of London frieze

Objectives
● To find out about houses in London at the time of the Great Fire.
● To describe key features of houses at this time.
● To produce pictures and models of 17th-century houses.

Vocabulary
timber, wood, thatch, window, door, chimney

Resources
Pictures, video material and reference books relating to 17th-century houses; art and craft materials, including paper and card of different colours, glue and paint.

Links
NC Design and technology KS1: (2a) to select tools, techniques and materials for making their product from a range suggested by the teacher; (2d) to assemble, join and combine materials and components. NC Art and design KS1: (2b) to try out tools and techniques.

Background
The Great Fire of London topic provides many possibilities for creative, practical work involving art and design. It is important to remember, however, that these activities should be underpinned by historical understanding. A key part of this lesson, for example, involves researching what 17th-century homes were like, so that their pictures and models have some historical accuracy.

Introduction
● Show pictures of London at the time of the fire in which timber framed buildings can be seen. Ask the children to note the key features of 17th-century buildings, such as their wooden construction, thatched roofs and the way they were built close together.
● Share the learning objectives with the children, emphasising that they will be working in small groups to produce large pictures of houses for a Great Fire of London frieze.

Main teaching activity
● Use pictures to look in detail at 17th-century houses in London. Cross-section drawings can be useful to help children understand how they were built with a wooden frame and plaster infill.
● Demonstrate how they can produce their own houses by drawing the outline shape on a large piece of cream paper. The timber framing can be added with strips of brown paper. Use black paper for doors and window frames, and straw-coloured paper for the roofs.
● Split the class into small groups and start them on the task. Provide visual references to guide them.
● An alternative for some groups might be to produce 3D models of houses, using boxes for the main shape, which could provide a foreground to the main frieze.

Plenary
● Review what the children have achieved by looking at their pictures, highlighting significant features
● Ask the children what else needs to be included in their frieze to make it look like the Great Fire of London. Encourage references to flames, people, and boats on the River Thames. These could all be added using appropriate materials, such as red and yellow paper foil for the flames.

Differentiation
Additional adult support is useful for this practical activity. More able children could be set further tasks to create other parts of the frieze.

Who was Samuel Pepys?

Objectives
● To find out about Samuel Pepys by looking at a portrait.
● To understand that Pepys lived long ago.
● To know that he was famous for writing a diary.
● To understand the importance of eyewitness accounts.

Vocabulary
Samuel Pepys, diary, portrait, eyewitness, feelings, rich, poor, clothing, hairstyle

Resources
Portrait of Pepys; reference books; websites on Pepys and the Great Fire of London (such as, www.channel4.com/history/microsites/H/history/fire/; www.bbc.co.uk/history/historic_figures/pepys_samuel.shtml); paper, pens and drawing materials.

Links
NC Art and design KS1: (5d) investigating different kinds of art, craft and design.
NC English KSI: En3 (1c) to put their ideas into sentences; (1d) to use a clear structure to organise their writing.

Background
Samuel Pepys lived from 1633 to 1703 and his diary spans the period from 1660 until 1669. His diary is an example of the importance of eyewitness accounts for finding out about events like the Great Fire. It provides a fascinating insight into his own life and the people of London. An educated and able person, Pepys was an important civil servant employed by the Admiralty. A portrait is a useful introduction to Pepys, allowing the children to use clues in the picture to make observations about his appearance, clothing and status in society.

Introduction
● Show the portrait of Pepys and ask the children to make brief comments about the picture.
● Tell the children that this is Samuel Pepys and he was an eyewitness to the fire. Explain the term 'eyewitness' and say that Pepys lived in London at the time of the Great Fire.
● Emphasise that the children will be looking at what the portrait tells us about Pepys.

Main teaching activity
● Ask the children what sort of picture this is. Encourage them to identify it as a painting and not a photograph. Introduce the term 'portrait' and explain it.
● Look carefully at the picture of Pepys. Discuss the details of his clothes, pointing out that these were fashionable at the time.
● Focus on his hairstyle and emphasise that this style was popular in the 17th century.
● Discuss how portraits can show a person's mood and feelings. Ask the children to describe Pepys' mood in the picture.
● Using the portrait, ask the children to say what kind of person they think Pepys is. Does he look rich, poor, important or ordinary?
● Ask the children to draw their own portrait of Samuel Pepys and to write some short sentences about his clothes, hairstyle, and the sort of person he was. Support this work with reference resources.

Plenary
● Show some of the portraits and ask the children to talk about them. Explain that Pepys is very famous because he wrote a detailed diary about events like the Great Fire. Discuss what a diary is and how this will be a focus for another lesson.

Differentiation
A writing framework with key questions could be used to support the children's written work. Less able children could draw the portrait and label it with the help of a wordbank. Encourage more able children to write fuller sentences.

The diary of Samuel Pepys

Objectives
- To find out about the Great Fire from Pepys' diary.
- To communicate their knowledge of the fire by making their own diary entries.
- To be aware of the importance of diaries as a genre.

Vocabulary
diary, Samuel Pepys, possessions, wine, Parmesan cheese, quill, ink, eyewitness, code

Resources
Portrait of Pepys, the photocopiable sheet 'The diary of Samuel Pepys' on page 139; pictures of the fire; reference books; word cards; modern diary; writing framework for diary entries; extract from the original diary showing shorthand code (optional); quill pen made from a feather; ink; pens and paper.

Links
NC English KS1: En3 (1a) to use adventurous and wide-ranging vocabulary; (1c) to put their ideas into sentences; (2b) to assemble and develop ideas on paper and on screen.
NLS Y2 T3 Text 20: to use texts read as models for own writing.

Background
The diary of Pepys provides a detailed account of the fire. Originally written in code, it would be useful to show the children what the real diary looks like and to introduce them to extracts of the original translation. For individual work, the children can use the simplified extracts on the photocopiable sheet. John Evelyn also recorded the fire in his diary and this could be used as an additional resource.

Introduction
- Show a modern diary to the children and identify what it is. Discuss the importance of diaries.
- Explain that to find out about the fire, we need to use information written by people who actually lived in London at the time and saw the Great Fire. Make reference to the term 'eyewitness'.
- Use the portrait to remind the children of Samuel Pepys and tell them that he wrote a famous diary that includes information about the fire.

Main teaching activity
- Read the extracts from the photocopiable sheet 'The diary of Samuel Pepys' on page 139, emphasising the dates.
- Ask the children what each sentence tells us about the fire. Emphasise key points, such as the large number of houses destroyed. Highlight how people like Pepys were keen to save their most valuable possessions.
- Invite the children to imagine that they were living in London at the time of the Great Fire, and to write their own diary entries, which they can illustrate with pictures.
- Use shared writing as a starting point to produce a few examples, such as: *I woke up early and opened my window.*
- Then let the children draft their own diary entries, using the writing framework. ICT can be used to facilitate the process of drafting and re-drafting.
- To support this activity word cards, pictures, reference books and website resources should be made available to provide some ideas.

Plenary
- Ask for volunteers to read out their diary entries.
- Conclude by asking the children what Pepys might have used to write his diary. Explain that he used a quill made from a large feather. Allow a few children to demonstrate writing with a quill and ink.

Differentiation
Less able children could be given the start of sentences to complete or diary entries with missing words. Encourage the more able children to write extended sentences with a range of vocabulary.

Fire-fighting today

Objectives
- To identify differences between fire-fighting now and at the time of the Great Fire.
- To be aware of people like firefighters who help us in the community.
- To know about the importance of preventing fires.

Vocabulary
fire station, fire officer, fire brigade, hose, fire engine, ladder, helmet, fire extinguisher

Resources
Fire service educational resources, such as fire-safety posters and pictures of fire-fighting today; digital camera.

Links
NC Citizenship KS1: (3g) rules for, and ways of, keeping safe and about people who can help them to stay safe; (5e) to meet and talk with people.

Background
It is important with a topic like the Great Fire to make comparisons with fire-fighting today. Visiting the local fire station or inviting a fire officer to the classroom is an excellent way of doing this. Careful liaison and preparation is necessary to ensure that any visit is appropriate for the children and to facilitate follow-up work. If you are taking the children out on a visit, extra adult support will be required. Wherever possible, create opportunities where the children can handle fire-service artefacts, such as a helmet. Possibilities for follow-up work include thinking about fire rules in school or at home and designing a fire-safety poster.

Introduction
- Tell the children that they will be finding out about fire-fighting today and how the fire service helps our community.
- Encourage the children to listen and observe carefully, whether you are visiting the fire station or having a visit from a fire officer.
- Ask the children to focus on the differences between fire-fighting now and at the time of the Great Fire.

Main teaching activity
- Whether visiting a fire station or having a classroom visit, children should be introduced to a number of themes, such as fire-fighting vehicles, equipment like powerful hoses and ladders, protective clothing, communications and fire safety.
- If possible, opportunities should be created for the children to handle different items, such as helmets.
- Encourage the children to ask questions about fire-fighting today. These could be identified by a structured discussion before the visit.
- If you are visiting a fire station, take photographs on a digital camera, so that specific reference can be made to what has been seen in a subsequent session.
- Children could compare fire-fighting in 1666 with the present day and also think about fire safety issues.

Plenary
- Ask the children to say what they have learned from the visit and how fire-fighting today is different from the time of the Great Fire. Can they think of a few ideas about how fires can be prevented?

Differentiation
Children of all abilities should be encouraged to ask questions during the session about fire-fighting. If a fire officer visits the classroom, some time could be allocated for the visitor to talk with the children in small groups in a more informal situation, allowing all the children to participate actively.

Escaping from the fire

Objectives
- To use pictures and eyewitness accounts to find out about the different ways people escaped from the fire.
- To use drama to tell the story of how people escaped from the fire.
- To understand some of the feelings and emotions of people involved in the Great Fire.

Vocabulary
River Thames, boat, smoke, heat, escape, valuables, cart, frightened, sparks, burning, crackling, hot, Pepys, rushing, crowds, crying

Resources
Painting and pictures of the Great Fire and people escaping; extracts from Pepys' diary (for example, the photocopiable sheet 'The diary of Samuel Pepys' on page 139); the photocopiable sheet 'Great Fire word cards' on page 140, one per group.

Links
NC English KS1: En1 (3a) to take turns in speaking; (4a) to use language and actions to explore and convey situations, characters and emotions.

Background
The Great Fire is a fascinating story offering plenty of potential for drama, which is an excellent way to promote speaking and listening as well as skills of historical enquiry and communication. The role play, however, needs to be based on sound historical understanding of the event, and so this lesson places a strong emphasis on exploring the actions and feelings of people escaping from the fire before letting the children plan their own scene. An alternative format would be to use hot-seating with each group in role as a family fleeing the fire and talking about their experiences.

Introduction
- Show a picture of the Great Fire with buildings burning and people escaping by boat on the River Thames.
- Ask the children to imagine that they were there at the time. What would they see? What would they hear? What would they smell? How would they feel? Discuss their responses, emphasising the smell of the smoke, the heat, the sounds of people shouting and the worry on their faces.
- Tell the children that they will be working in groups to plan and present a short role play about escaping from the fire.

Main teaching activity
- Using your pictures and extracts from the diary of Pepys, discuss what actions people took when faced by the fire.
- List possible responses, such as collecting together some possessions and escaping by walking, using a cart or taking a boat. Encourage discussion of other actions, for example, burying valuables in the garden or seeking shelter in a stone building like a church. Emphasise how people would be very frightened, especially children.
- Split the class into small groups and ask them to plan out a short piece of drama. As a starting point, write their ideas on the board and use the photocopiable sheet 'Great Fire word cards' on page 140 to support the activity.

Plenary
- Ask groups to present their role play. Encourage other groups to say what each role-play says about the Great Fire.
- Explain that, although the fire was a terrible thing, only a few people died because of it. Can the children suggest why?

Differentiation
Children can share their skills and ideas in mixed-ability groups. Groups will need to be individually supported and guided to maintain focus. Children may need help in structuring the role play to match suitable words with actions.

A timeline of the fire

Objectives
● To place events of the fire in the correct chronological order.
● To introduce children to a timeline of the Great Fire.
● To know and be able to talk about the main events of the fire.

Vocabulary
timeline, date, days of the week, September

Resources
The photocopiable sheet 'A timeline of the Great Fire' on page 141, one per child; scissors; glue; paper or workbooks; a Great Fire timeline (including the dates of the fire from Sunday 2 September 1666 to Friday 7 September 1666); pictures of different stages of the fire.

Links
NC ICT KS1: (1a) to gather information from a variety of sources.
NC Mathematics KS1: Ma2 (2c) to read and write numbers to 20.

Background
Developing chronological understanding is an important part of Key Stage 1 History and can be promoted by children making their own simple timelines of the fire. With the fire lasting only a matter of days, children can relate easily to a timeline that focuses on a single week. Using pictures should allow the children to sequence the events correctly and provides opportunity for them to tell the story of the fire themselves. This activity can be valuable for assessing their historical sequencing skills and knowledge of events.

Introduction
● Show a few pictures of events that took place during the Great Fire. Ask the children to explain what they show and suggest a title for each picture, such as: *The fire starts at a baker's shop in Pudding Lane.* Ask them to sequence the pictures chronologically.
● Introduce a blank timeline of the Great Fire covering the period from Sunday 2 September until Friday 7 September. Ask the children to say where the pictures should go on the timeline.
● Count how many days the fire lasted.
● Explain to the children that they will be making their own time line, using pictures and text.

Main teaching activity
● Give out a copy of the photocopiable sheet 'A timeline of the Great Fire' on page 141 to each child. Ask the children to cut out the pictures, captions and dates.
● Let the children work in pairs to start with, discussing each picture and matching it with the correct title.
● Once they have completed this task, ask the children to work on their own timelines of the Great Fire. Encourage them to sequence their pictures chronologically and to glue them into their books.
● Invite the children to retell the story of the fire by talking about the pictures as this will reinforce their learning about the Great Fire and also their understanding of chronological order.

Plenary
● Together check the children's timelines. Have they put all the pictures and captions in the correct order?
● Emphasise the importance of time in history and the use of dates by which events can be sequenced.

Differentiation
The more able children could be given additional pictures to add to their timeline. Less able children might need help with the cutting and sorting out the timeline layout before gluing and extra adult support will be useful.

A newspaper report

Objectives
- To know that the fire destroyed large parts of London.
- To understand how people were affected by the fire.
- To recognise a newspaper as a genre.
- To be aware that disasters still occur today.

Vocabulary
newspaper, headlines, water squirt, gunpowder, ashes, ruins, homeless, disaster

Resources
Timeline of the fire (see Lesson 9 on page 132); pictures of different stages of the fire; example of a newspaper front page, perhaps showing a disaster; pictures of modern-day disasters and resulting homelessness (optional); newspaper template, one per pair of children; pens and pencils.

Links
NC ICT KS1: (3a) to share their ideas by presenting information in a variety of forms; (3b) to present their completed work effectively.
NC English KS1: En2 (7a) include print and ICT based information texts, including those with continuous text and relevant illustrations.
NLS Y2 T3 Text 20: to use texts read as models for own writing.

Background
Children need to be made aware of the huge physical damage to London as a result of the fire: over 13,000 houses and 87 churches were destroyed. It is estimated that about 100,000 people lost their homes and were forced to stay in tents or rough shelters, many camping on Hampstead Heath. Fortunately, few people died as a result of the fire, although families often faced financial ruin having lost all their goods and possessions.

Introduction
- On your timeline, show when the Great Fire started and spread.
- Discuss reasons why the fire could not be stopped, such as the wooden houses, the wind and the poor fire-fighting methods.
- Use a picture to illustrate how buildings were blown up, using gunpowder to create firebreaks.
- By Thursday the fire had begun to die down. Ask the children to think of other reasons why the fire ended. Explain how the weather changed and the wind became less strong.
- Tell the children they will be investigating how the fire affected London and its people.

Main teaching activity
- Using a picture of the burned out city, ask the children to imagine walking through the buildings. What would they see, smell and hear? List their ideas on the board. Mention that Samuel Pepys wrote in his diary about the ashes being so hot that they burned his shoes!
- Focus on the people made homeless by the fire. Links could be made to modern-day disasters, such as earthquakes, where people lose their homes.
- Give the children factual information about the fire. Emphasise that, although few people died, huge damage was done.
- Ask the children to work in pairs to produce a newspaper front page written at the end of the Great Fire. Ensure that they recognise the key features of a newspaper. It may be useful to provide a template, with spaces for headlines, a short story and pictures.
- Encourage the children to focus on how the fire went out of control, the damage it did and the people who were made homeless.

Plenary
- Review the progress made by the children and discuss examples of their work. What do they tell the reader about the Great Fire?

Differentiation
The less able could be paired together for this activity and be given extra support. The use of ICT would help all children, by allowing drafting and correcting and encouraging good quality presentation.

London's burning!

Objectives
● To know key words relating to the Great Fire.
● To develop an understanding of rhymes.
● To write a short poem about the Great Fire.

Vocabulary
London, burning, fire, water, engine, sparks, smoke, flame, hot

Resources
Large version of 'London's Burning'; paper, pens and pencils; art materials.

Links
NC Music KS1: (1a) to use their voices expressively by singing songs and speaking chants and rhymes.
NC English KS1: En2 (6a) include stories and poems with familiar settings; (6g) texts where the use of language benefits from being read aloud.
NC English KS1: En3 (12) the range of forms of writing and reading should include poems.
NLS Y1 T1 Text 10: to use rhymes as models for their own writing; Y1 T2 Text 11: to learn and recite simple rhymes, with actions; Y2 T2 Text 15: to use structures from poems as basis for writing.

Background
The use of rhymes or songs like 'London's Burning' is very important at Key Stage 1, promoting an understanding of rhyme and rhythm as well as introducing new vocabulary. Moreover, rhymes are also important for communicating historical information as 'London's Burning' illustrates:

> London's burning, London's burning,
> Fetch the engine, fetch the engine,
> Fire! Fire! Fire! Fire!
> Pour on water, pour on water.

Introduction
● Show the children the words of the rhyme 'London's Burning' and ask them what it is about. Discuss links with the Great Fire of 1666.
● Sing the rhyme a few times with the children. Ask them to suggest actions to go with the rhyme and sing it again with the actions.
● Share learning objectives, emphasising that the lesson will focus on important words about the fire which the children can use to write their own short poem or rhyme about the Great Fire.

Main teaching activity
● Look in detail at the text of 'London's Burning' and what it means. Highlight key words, such as *London*, *burning*, *fire*, *water* and *engine*. Do they know what an engine might be?
● Now encourage the children to think of other words linked to the Great Fire by asking them to talk about what they would have seen, heard and smelled, if they had been a witness to the fire. Write the words on the board or use pre-prepared word cards.
● Tell the children that they are going to write a short poem about the Great Fire. Work with the class to write a few lines as examples.
● Let the children start writing their poem. Encourage them to draft and re-draft their work.
● Having written their poem, ask the children to surround the text with pictures that convey the idea of fire, such as: flames, smoke and sparks. Poems could be presented in a shape format, such as a fire bucket or a burning house.

Plenary
● Ask for volunteers to read out their poems.
● Reinforce their knowledge of the vocabulary by showing word cards and asking children to explain their meaning.

Differentiation
● The less able children could be grouped to work with the teacher or classroom assistant and produce some shared writing for their poem. Encourage more able children to write slightly longer poems.

Rebuilding London

Objectives
- To find out about the rebuilding of London.
- To understand how London was rebuilt and the role of Sir Christopher Wren.
- To know about the building of St Paul's Cathedral and The Monument.

Vocabulary
Sir Christopher Wren, architect, St Paul's Cathedral, results, King Charles II, stone, brick, The Monument

Resources
Map and picture of the damaged city; pictures, videos, reference books and websites about Sir Christopher Wren, St Paul's Cathedral, The Monument and the rebuilding of London; the photocopiable sheet 'The rebuilding of London' on page 142.

Links
NC Art and design KS1: (5d) investigate different kinds of art, craft and design.

Background
An interesting aspect of the Great Fire is what subsequently happened in London, notably the rebuilding of the city. Other important results included the growth of the insurance business and the decline of the plague. At Key Stage 1 the work of Sir Christopher Wren and the building of St Paul's Cathedral (1675-1710) provides a good focus. Although the eventual rebuilding of London did not match King Charles' ambitions to rival Paris, much progress was made by widening streets, creating attractive squares and rebuilding in brick, stone and tile instead of wood and thatch.

Introduction
- Ask the children to talk briefly in pairs about how the Great Fire affected London. List suggestions on the board.
- Highlight the fact that many buildings had burned down and large areas of the city were destroyed. Illustrate this with a picture and a map showing the spread of the fire.
- Ask the children to suggest what happened in London after the fire to introduce the idea of rebuilding. Explain that they will be finding out about how London was rebuilt and about Sir Christopher Wren.

Main teaching activity
- Emphasise that rebuilding took a long time and was difficult. Nobody wanted another fire, and therefore, rules were laid down for the rebuilding to stop future fires spreading easily. Ask the children to think of a few of these rules, such as the use of brick or stone, wider streets and houses built further apart.
- Tell the story of the rebuilding of London, using text and pictures.
- Talk about King Charles II, who wanted a grand rebuilding to imitate Paris. Discus the term 'architect' and refer to the work of Sir Christopher Wren. Focus on the building of St Paul's Cathedral.
- Ask the children to list the differences between living in London before and after the fire.
- Give the children time to complete the activities on the photocopiable sheet 'The rebuilding of London' on page 142.

Plenary
- Discuss the children's answers, reinforcing key points about the rebuilding of London.
- Conclude by showing a picture of The Monument, designed by Wren to commemorate the Great Fire and built close to the site of the bakery where the fire started.

Differentiation
Differentiate the questions, with simpler, direct questions for less able children and more open-ended ones for more able children.

A Great Fire of London quiz

Objectives
● To find out about the Great Fire by using a variety of sources.
● To ask and answer questions about the fire.

Vocabulary
quiz, Great Fire, Samuel Pepys, diary, Charles II, the Stuarts, Sir Christopher Wren, St Paul's Cathedral

Resources
Reference books and pictures of the Great Fire; access to relevant websites and CD-ROMs; drawing materials or ICT art package and computers.

Background
In a concluding session it is important to provide an opportunity to revise important aspects of the topic, and a quiz is one approach. In primary history work, it is good practice for children themselves to identify historical questions and the group activity in this lesson allows them to do so. Giving children an opportunity to communicate their understanding and views of the Great Fire in pictorial form will no doubt produce a range of interesting and diverse outcomes which can form the basis of a display.

Introduction
● Tell the children that they will be having a quiz about the Great Fire of London. Ask for volunteers to explain what a quiz is.
● Say that a list of questions is needed for a quiz and explain that they will be working in teams to identify questions which can then be asked to the other groups.
● Introduce the children to the resources, such as the books and websites.

Main teaching activity
● Ask the class to suggest some questions about the Great Fire. Encourage questions that are reasonably specific, rather than open ended, such as: *In which street did the fire start? What did Pepys bury in his garden?*
● Split the class into groups and start them on their research. Careful support and guidance will be necessary to ensure that they identify suitable questions and that they know the answers!
● Ask the groups to record their questions and answers. Assess these for suitability, overlap and fairness.
● Bring the class together and start the quiz. The format can vary depending on ability. Each group, for example, could ask two questions to the other teams who could respond orally or in writing. It is important that the group asking the question has the opportunity to say whether the answer is correct and, if not, what the answer is.
● Use a scorecard to add more interest and a competitive element.
● The topic could be concluded by asking the children to produce a coloured picture, representing their own view of the Great Fire.

Links
NC Art and design KS1: (2c) to represent observations, ideas and feelings, and design and make images and artefacts. NC English KS1: En1 (3a) to join in as members of a group and to take turns in speaking.

Plenary
● Discuss with the children what they have learned about the Great Fire of London and which parts of the topic they have enjoyed most.

Differentiation
The use of mixed-ability groups should encourage the sharing of skills and ideas. Careful support will need to be given to groups to encourage all pupils to participate actively.

The start of the Great Fire

◼ Label this picture of Thomas Farynor's bakery using the following words.

| oven | wood | paddle | bags of flour | bread | fire |

What do you think it would be like working in this bakery? _____

_____

Apart from bread, what else could the bakery have made? _____

_____

◼ What is used in your own home today for baking? Draw a picture of this and give it a title.

_____

◼ List a few differences between baking at home today and Farynor's bakery on the back of this sheet.

Why did the Great Fire spread so fast?

This picture shows London burning during the Great Fire. The fire spread very quickly after it started in the bakery.

🔲 Use the word cards to help you to write about why this happened.

wooden houses	flames blown by strong winds	narrow streets
buckets of water	houses close together	roofs made of straw

■SCHOLASTIC

The diary of Samuel Pepys

Samuel Pepys lived in London at the time of the Great Fire and these are some of the things he wrote in his diary in September 1666.

Sunday 2 September

Jane came and told me that over 300 houses had been burned down during the night and that the fire was now burning by London Bridge.

Poor people stayed in their houses until the fire almost touched them and then ran to the boats.

I saw some poor pigeons which hovered near the fire until some of them burned their wings and fell down.

I told the King and Duke of York what I had seen and that, unless the King ordered houses to be pulled down, nothing could stop the fire.

I walked along Watling Street and saw many people trying to escape the fire with goods carried in carts or on their backs.

Monday 3 September

At 4 o'clock in the morning I packed my money, silver and best things into a cart and moved it to Bethnal Green to keep safe at a friend's house.

Tuesday 4 September

I dug a hole in the garden of my house to bury my wine and Parmesan cheese for safe keeping.

Wednesday 5 September

With the blowing up of houses and the great help of workmen from the King's dockyard, the fire is being stopped.

Friday 7 September

I got up at 5 o'clock in the morning and, blessed be God, found that all was well. (The fire had gone out.)

I saw all the town burned and the miserable sight of Paul's church with all the roofs fallen.

Great Fire word cards

smoke	flames
boat	carry
cart	burning
bury	hurry
crowds	valuables
crying	belongings
river	Thames
heat	tired
frightened	boatman

A timeline of the Great Fire

◼ Cut out the pictures, captions and dates. Match them up and put them in the right order.

◼ Put the dates at the start and end. Stick them all in your book to make a timeline.

People escape from the fire.	Pepys gives advice to the King.
The fire is out of control.	Buildings are blown up.
The start of the fire.	Friday 7 September 1666
The end of the fire.	Sunday 2 September 1666

The rebuilding of London

This picture shows London when it was rebuilt after the Great Fire.

🔲 Use the wordbank to complete this story about the rebuilding of London.

King _____ wanted London to be rebuilt like _____ with large

_____ buildings, wide _____ and parks. An _____ was needed

to draw up plans and Christopher Wren was chosen. There was not enough

_____ for London to be rebuilt as the King wanted but many

improvements were made. _____ became very famous for building St Paul's

_____ which was finished in 1710. Near _____ Lane where the

fire started, _____ _____ was built to remember the _____ _____.

cathedral	stone	money	architect	The Monument
Charles	Pudding	Great	Paris	Fire	streets	Wren

📖 S C H O L A S T I C

CHAPTER 8

Remembrance Day

This chapter supports Unit 17 'What are we remembering on Remembrance Day?' of the QCA Scheme of Work for History. Remembrance Day is on 11 November, commemorating the end of the First World War. Remembrance Sunday is held on the nearest Sunday to 11 November, with usually a minute's silence at 11am. It has now become a time to remember all those who have given their lives in wartime during and since the First World War.

Children will have seen people wearing poppies at this time of year and so they will be naturally curious about the reason for this. An activity on making poppies enables the children to begin work on this sensitive topic by relating to something familiar. The photocopiable resources also support the lessons with texts relating to the First World War in the form of a poem and diary extract.

	OBJECTIVES	MAIN ACTIVITY
Lesson 1	To use objects to find out about the past. To know that symbols can be used to commemorate events.	Children learn about the reasons for wearing poppies. They complete artwork and a short piece of writing.
Lesson 2 🅟	To communicate their knowledge of history through art.	Using templates on the photocopiable sheet, children make their own poppies.
Lesson 3	To find out about the past from pictures of historic sites. To ask and answer questions about the past.	Children investigate pictures of war memorials. They make their own drawings and label them.
Lesson 4	To find out about the past from historic sites.	Children are taken on a visit to see a war memorial. They take notes and make sketches.
Lesson 5	To find out about the past from written sources.	Learning to understand the text on a memorial leads the children to reconstruct it in child-friendly language. They draw pictures.
Lesson 6	To place events in chronological order. To use common words and phrases related to the passing of time.	Children create a timeline to show when the First and Second World Wars took place.
Lesson 7 🅟	To find out about the past from oral accounts. To ask and answer questions about the past.	Listening to someone's memories encourages children to consider the importance of remembrance. They complete a grid using the information they have heard.
Lesson 8 🅟	To find out about the past from oral and written accounts.	Children read a wartime account written by a soldier and make a picture list of what they learn.
Lesson 9 🅟	To find out about the past from poems. To communicate their knowledge of history in a variety of ways.	After sharing a poem about the First World War, the children write a poem of their own about one of their memories.
Lesson 10	To find out about the past from a range of sources. To ask and answer questions about the past.	Children use the internet to discover information about Remembrance Day and to answer their own questions.
Lesson 11 🅟	To communicate their knowledge of history through role play.	After listening to a First World War poem or account, the children set up a role-play area and mime parts of the text.
Lesson 12	To communicate their knowledge of history in a variety of ways.	Children take part in an assembly for Remembrance Day.

Poppies

Background
Partly because of the popularity of the poem 'In Flanders Fields', written by John McCrae during the First World War, the poppy was adopted as the symbol of remembrance for those killed in the wars from Britain, France, the United States, Canada, Australia and other Commonwealth countries. It was also a symbol of hope as it had survived the devastation of war in the fields.

Young children will be initially interested in this topic because of its relevance to things they see around them; the Poppy Day appeal, as a regular annual event, is bound to arouse their curiosity. This topic will help the children to understand why the flower is used as a symbol.

Introduction
● Display the selection of poppies , including the Remembrance Day poppies.
● Discuss with the children where they have seen these before.

Main teaching activity
● Point out the Remembrance Day poppies. Do the children know why people wear them?
● Talk about the reasons for wearing these on Poppy Day (another name for Remembrance Day).
● Show them the pictures of the fields following the battles of the First World War, and ask the children what they can see (for example, poppies growing in the fields).
● Talk about how some fields were red with the colour of the poppies and how this made people think about all the blood that had been spilled in the fighting during the war.
● Explain how the poppy has been used to commemorate and help everyone remember the people who died in the First World War and, then later on, in the two World Wars.
● Talk about other important events that we remember, such as religious festivals, and look at symbols that represent these, such as candles for Christian and Jewish festivals.
● Provide the children with materials to complete artwork and a short piece of writing, such as labels or short sentences, about poppies.
● Ask the children to draw a poppy, label it, and write a short sentence to describe what the poppy helps us to remember and why.

Plenary
● Review the children's drawings and writing, and help them make a wall display of their work.

Differentiation
Provide a wordbank to support less able writers. The more able children should be encouraged to write full or extended sentences.

Making a poppy field

Objectives
● To communicate their knowledge of history through art.

Vocabulary
remember, soldiers, killed, cornfield

Resources
Picture of a Belgian poppy field; enlarged pictures of poppies; large strip of green or golden frieze paper on the wall as the background of a green field or cornfield for the finished poppies; the photocopiable sheet 'Making your own poppy' on page 156, one per child; coloured crayons, pastels or paints; scissors; glue; green paper or pipe cleaners; completed poppy for demonstration purposes; cards for captions.

Links
NC English KS1: En1 (1) to speak clearly and with confidence; (2) to listen and respond to others. NC ICT KS1: (2a) to use images to develop ideas. NC Design and technology KS1: (2d) to assemble, join and combine materials and components.

Background
The poppy grows abundantly in the fields of Flanders in western Belgium where most of the fighting took place during the First World War. Following the war, the red of the poppies covering the fields made people, such as John McCrae, think about the blood of all the soldiers that had been spilled in those fields.

Introduction
● Show the children pictures of poppy fields in Belgium.
● Tell the children why these poppy fields are significant and what they remind people of. Refer back to what the children learned in Lesson 1 (on page 144).
● Say to the children that they are going to make paper poppies to create a wall display.

Main teaching activity
● Show the children enlarged pictures of real poppies so that they can see what colours they will need.
● Organise the children to work in small groups and give out the art materials and copies of the photocopiable sheet 'Making your own poppy' on page 156.
● Show the class how to colour in and cut out the templates from their photocopiable sheet. Encourage them to colour in the petals using different shades and to use black for the centre.
● Demonstrate with one poppy how to add more petals. The narrow ends of the petals should be glued together and then covered by the black centre. The petals can be folded outwards to create a 3D effect.
● Help the children to make their own poppies. Strips of green paper or green pipe cleaners can be used for the stems, and the photocopiable sheet includes a template for a leaf.
● Support the children in the activity as necessary, especially with the cutting and gluing.

Plenary
● Ask the children to come out one at a time and stick their poppy on to the green or golden background previously put up on the wall. This background can be used as a backdrop or centrepiece for any other work the children produce or for displays used during the course of the topic.

Differentiation
Extra adult support will be needed for children with special needs during this activity to help with the cutting out, making and gluing together of the poppies. Ask more able children to write short sentences or captions to stick under the poppies. Include information on why poppies are used for Remembrance Day.

Pictures of war memorials

Objectives
● To find out about the past from pictures of historic sites.
● To ask and answer questions about the past.

Vocabulary
memorial, monument, First World War, Second World War

Resources
Collection of pictures of war memorials; drawing and writing materials.

Links
NLS Y1-2 Word level work: vocabulary extension by using words linked to a particular topic; Y1 T2 Text 22: to write labels; Text 23 to write captions.
NC English KS1: En1 (1) to speak clearly and with confidence; (2) to listen and respond to others.
NC Art and design KS1: (2c) to represent observations and make images.

Background
War memorials can be found in most towns and villages in Britain. They usually commemorate the deaths of people killed during both the First and Second World Wars. This topic will therefore have real meaning for young children through its connection with everyday life.

Introduction
● Explain the lesson objectives to the class and tell them that they are going to look at some pictures of memorials.
● Make sure that all the children have a good understanding of the meaning of the term 'memorial' (for example, a special monument or place which helps us to remember something important that has happened in the past).
● Encourage the children to note the similarity between the words 'remember' and 'memorial'. Write both words on the board or on cards to create a wordbank.

Main teaching activity
● Show the class pictures of a number of different war memorials and ask the children to study the pictures carefully. What do they notice? Do the structures have common features?
● Discuss why they were built and when. If possible, read the inscriptions on the memorials out loud and discuss what these mean.
● Use questions to prompt the children to think about why memorials are important, such as: *What are memorials? Where do we see them? What are they for? When were they built? What is written on them?*
● Ask the children to choose their favourite picture of a war memorial and to make a large drawing of it of their own.
● Once they have finished their picture, encourage the children to write labels or captions for their drawings.

Plenary
● Share the children's pictures and captions with the class, and discuss the features they show.
● Ask the children to help you create a display of the pictures, or add them to the frieze created in Lesson 2 (on page 145).
● Recap that war memorials are important because they help us to remember people from a particular town who died in the First or Second World War.

Differentiation
More able children should be encouraged to write extended sentences or captions to accompany their pictures. For less able children, spend more time examining and identifying the features of a war memorial before they begin the drawing exercise. They will also need more support when writing their labels.

Visit to a war memorial

Objectives
● To find out about the past from historic sites.

Vocabulary
visit, names, inscription, statues

Resources
Photographs of a local war memorial; map of the town, locating the memorial and the school; sketching and note-making materials; a camera.

Links
NLS: Y1 T2 Sentence 7: to use capital letters for names; Y2 T2 Sentence 9: to secure the use of simple sentences; Y2 T3 Text 19: to make simple notes from non-fiction texts.
NC Art and design KS1: (1a) to record from first-hand observation.

Background
Advance preparation is key to a successful field trip. Identify a local memorial and organise a short visit to look at this. Visit the memorial beforehand to ascertain its date and the particular war that it commemorates. Make a note of its features, such as carvings, figures or inscriptions, and plan key questions for the children. Take a variety of photographs, some close-up so that the writing can be seen as clearly as possible. Make a note of any potential hazards for risk assessment. Enlist additional adult support. Meet with them to discuss the organisation and purpose of the visit, and provide brief notes about your objectives, the main activities of the day and their role during the visit. Suggest ways of working with the children such as note-making or scribing for the less able children, and questioning and extending the more able.

Introduction
● Before the trip, discuss the learning objective. What does a memorial tell us about war?
● Show the pictures of the memorial and focus on its main features. Point out where it is on a map of the town.
● Talk about the reasons why this memorial was built.
● Remind the children about the importance of good behaviour on the visit.

Main teaching activity
● On arrival at the memorial, divide the class into smaller groups each accompanied by an adult. Remind the children of the learning objective.
● Look at the writing on the memorial. Can the children tell you then this memorial was built?
● Discuss what the inscriptions on the memorial represent.
● Set key questions or tasks for the children. Some could focus on what the memorial looks like and others could focus on the inscriptions.
● Allow the class time to make sketches and take photographs. Ask the adult helpers to assist the children in copying some of the inscriptions and names.

Plenary
● Briefly discuss what the children have observed. Collect all the work that has been done for follow-up activities in school.

Differentiation
The most able children will be able to make notes and write short pieces of prose about the key points they have noticed. Less able and younger children will need adult support in making notes and sketches and identifying key features.

Reading and writing inscriptions

Objectives
● To find out about the past from written sources.

Vocabulary
writing, words, names, dates

Resources
Enlarged copy of the text photographed or copied from a war memorial; art materials.

Background
The texts that children will see on memorials will have been written with adult readers in mind. It may also be written in script that is difficult for young children to read. This lesson, therefore, focuses on the skills needed to read and interpret such inscriptions. You may wish to use the text on the memorial that you visited with the class (see Lesson 4 on page 147) or you may wish to use another one to extend the children's knowledge of different memorials.

Introduction
● Remind the children of their visit to a war memorial and what they learned from it.
● Display an enlarged copy of the text from a war memorial.
● Look at the text with the class, reviewing with them the type of writing it includes, such as verses, lines of poetry, lists of names, dates and so on.

Main teaching activity
● Read the text from the memorial carefully with the class and identify new and unusual words to add to a class wordbank.
● Note the different types of writing the memorial includes, such as verses, lines of poetry, lists of names and dates.
● Ask the children what the writing from the memorial says. What information is given in the text?
● Discuss why the memorial is written in this way. Is the inscription difficult to read or to understand? Could they write it in simpler language?
● Work with the class in a shared writing session to reconstruct the text in child-friendly language.
● Provide art materials for the children to draw the memorial with the revised version of the text on it.

Plenary
● Re-read the revised text with the whole class. Ask the children if they think this would be a better text to have on the memorial, or do they prefer the original? Can they give you reasons for their choice?
● Help the children to create a display of the memorial with the original text and the children's drawings with the revised wording.

Links
NLS Y1-2 Word level work: vocabulary extension by using words linked to a particular topic.
NC English KS1: En2 (1j) to decipher new words, and confirm their meaning.
NC English KS1: En3 (1e) to vary their writing to suit the purpose and reader.

Differentiation
Carefully differentiate questioning to suit the children's abilities. Less able children will need more support in understanding and reading the text on the memorial. More able children could be encouraged to write a line or two of their own revised version of the text.

A simple timeline

Objectives
● To place events in chronological order.
● To use common words and phrases related to the passing of time.

Vocabulary
timeline, date, label

Resources
Large timeline for the classroom wall; cards for labels, phrases and dates; pens; tape or thread.

Background
Timelines are a useful way of making an abstract idea into something real for young children to see and understand. At Key Stage 1 it is important to keep any timeline activity simple and free from complicated details and dates. By the upper stages of Key Stage 1, however, the more able children will begin to understand the importance of dates and how they work.

Introduction
● Talk about what the children know about the two World Wars, the soldiers and the reason for people wanting to wear poppies today.
● Review these ideas with them, for example, people wear poppies as a way of remembering all the soldiers who died in the wars.
● Discuss how the poppy became a symbol of remembrance, following the poem of John McCrae. Read the poem to the children, if they have not heard it before. You can find a copy of the poem on the website: www.spartacus.schoolnet.co.uk/FWWmccrae.htm.

Main teaching activity
● Talk about when the First World War and the Second World War took place.
● Prompt the children with questions such as: *When were the two World Wars? How do we know about them? How can we show when they happened?*
● Use a simple timeline to show when the two wars took place. Ask for volunteers to come out and add the dates of the wars to the line, and discuss what the dates mean, comparing them with today's date.
● Mark the periods of the wars, using tape or thread to cover the number of years in each case.
● Discuss with the class how long each war lasted. Compare these time spans with the ages of the children in your class to give them some way of comparing the lengths of time.
● Ask the children how we know when the wars took place, for example: from accounts, documents, books and photographs.

Plenary
● Invite the children to suggest other information, such as events, people, festivals, and their own birthdays, that they might remember or know about. Complete simple labels on the cards provided for addition to the timeline. It will be useful here to have some ideas of your own to demonstrate how dates can be added.

Links
NLS Y1-2 Text level work: writing composition: to organise information into charts.
NNS Y2: to read and write whole numbers to at least 100.

Differentiation
During the plenary activity, less able children will need extra support and prompting for ideas to add to the timeline. Encourage more able and older children to write their own labels to add to the timeline.

Our families' memories

Background
This activity can be used in two ways: either to explore memory and
remembrance generally or to look more specifically at particular
memories, for example, those of the Second World War. You could use
simple accounts of your own family life or, alternatively, invite a guest
to talk about their memories relating to the Second World War.
Listening to a visitor or to their own teacher speaking about their
memories will fascinate young children. It will also motivate them to
talk about their own memories, developing their understanding of the
concept of remembering and remembrance at the same time. The aim
of this activity is to emphasise the importance of remembrance for
important events. It would be useful to brief the visitor about this
objective to give them a focus for their talk.

Introduction
● Introduce the topic for the lesson and share the lesson objectives
with the children.
● Ask the class questions, such as: *What are memories? What
memories do we all have?*
● Tell the children that, during the talk, they will be asking some
questions of their own.
● Encourage them to suggest questions and to write them down.

Main teaching activity
● Either use your own memories of family life or invite a guest to talk
about their memories, including those to do with the war.
● Whether it is you or a visitor speaking, concentrate on areas that
would be interesting for young children, such as childhood, different
food, birthday parties, toys, holidays, home and favourite things.
● Encourage the children to think of suitable questions to ask.
● Record the question and answer session, either using a camcorder
or tape recorder.
● Give the children a copy each of the photocopiable sheet
'Remembering the Second World War' on page 157 to complete.

Plenary
● The children will enjoy listening again to their questions and the
answers given once the visitor has left, or as a conclusion to the
lesson. Review together what the children have written on their grids.
● Talk about how people can have both happy and sad memories, and
relate this idea to remembering the wars.

Differentiation
Encourage the more able children to devise some more searching
questions and to write down the answers in full sentences on their
grid. Less able children will need support in completing the grid.

Soldier's memories

Objectives
● To find out about the past from oral and written accounts.

Vocabulary
account, memories, oral, written

Resources
Big books or books about memory, such as *Wilfrid Gordon McDonald Partridge* by Mem Fox (Puffin Books); the photocopiable sheet 'A soldier's account' on page 158, one per child.

Links
NLS Y2 T 3 Text 13: to understand the distinction between fact and fiction. NC Art and design KS1: (2c) to represent observations and make images.

Background
This lesson provides an opportunity to link the past with children's own experiences and with books about memories. From hearing and reading the first-hand accounts, the children can also begin to appreciate the difference between real accounts and fictional accounts of the past.

Introduction
● Discuss the meaning of 'memory', and ask the children: *What happy and sad memories do we have?* Encourage them to talk about some of their own memories, some recent and some from long ago.
● Ask them what can be learned from people's memories.
● Explain the lesson objectives and tell the children that they are going to learn a little about what it was like in wartime from reading something written by a soldier who was there at the time.

Main teaching activity
● Give each of the children a copy of the photocopiable sheet 'A soldier's account' on page 158. Read the account together and encourage the children to think about what it was like to be in a war.
● Talk about any words that may be unfamiliar to the children (for example, 'Boche' was a derogatory French slang word meaning 'blockhead' that was used in wartime to refer to the German enemy).
● Discuss with the class which they think are happy memories and which are sad memories that the soldier is remembering. Ask the children what they have learned from hearing or reading them.
● Point out the details given in the account and what they tell us about the First World War. Explain what the trenches were and how soldiers had to put up with some very unpleasant conditions in them.
● Encourage the children to say what they think the trenches looked and sounded like from the account.
● Ask the children to make a picture list of the things they have learned or found out from reading the account. Invite volunteers to share their list with the rest of the class.

Plenary
● Share a Big Book or story with the class, such as *Wilfred Gordon McDonald Partridge* by Mem Fox. Talk about the different kinds of memories people can have. Discuss the difference between real accounts and stories that have been made up, like the ones in the book by Mem Fox.

Differentiation
More able children will be able to annotate their picture lists, while children from a younger age group or less able children may need prompting to help them recall some of the things they found out.

Memories in poems

Objectives
● To find out about the past from poems.
● To communicate their knowledge of history in a variety of ways.

Vocabulary
poem, verse, shells

Resources
The photocopiable sheet 'A poem from the First World War' on page 159, one per child and one enlarged for display; other war poems suited to the children's ability; writing and drawing materials.

Background
Poems written during the First World War are generally unsuitable for young children, however, some are understandable. 'Bombardment' tells us about the terrifying conditions the soldiers lived in, evoking the fear and tension they must have felt while being bombed in the trenches.

Introduction
● Explain to the children that they will be reading poems to learn about the First World War.
● Ask the children if they have heard a war poem before. Tell them that a lot of the poems were written by soldiers in the war, so they knew what life was really like in the trenches.

Main teaching activity
● Choose a suitable poem or selected verses from a poem written about war or you can use the poem 'Bombardment' on the photocopiable sheet on page 159.
● Read the poem or verses with the children and discuss what the lines describe (for example, soldiers feeling afraid in 'Bombardment'). Talk about what the title of the poem means.
● In 'Bombardment', ask the children what picture is given by the poet. You may find it helpful to create a simple timeline to illustrate what happens over the period of five days.
● Talk about the children's own memories of events from the past – either recent memories or from longer ago. This might be about a birthday party or a holiday, for example. Have a few memories of your own ready as a starting point for the discussion.
● Write some lines on the board, as a shared-writing activity, to show the children how to create a simple poem.
● Provide the children with a wordbank of suitable words.
● Hand out pens or pencils and paper, and encourage the children to write a few lines about one of their own memories.
● Give the children drawing materials and encourage the children to illustrate their verses.

Links
NLS Y2 T2 Text 15: to use structures from poems as a basis for writing.
NLS Y2 T3 Text 13: to understand the distinction between fact and fiction.
NC Art and design KS1: (2c) to represent observations and make images.

Plenary
● Ask for volunteers to share some of their poems with the rest of the class.
● Work with the children to make a display of the poems and illustrations.

Differentiation
Less able writers will need adult support when composing their verses. The most able children could write about a memory from the topic, for example, the class visit to the war memorial.

Finding out about Remembrance Day

Objectives
● To find out about the past from a range of sources.
● To ask and answer questions about the past.

Vocabulary
internet, website, web page

Resources
List of questions to prompt the children in their search for information; reference books; paper and pens; computers, one per pair; suitable web pages, pre-selected for the lesson, for example: www.woodlands-junior.kent.sch.uk/customs/Remembrance.html; www.bbc.co.uk/religion/remembrance/history/; www.cerneabbas.dorset.sch.uk/cas_remembrance.htm

Links
NLS Y2 T3 Text 14: to pose questions and record these in writing; Y2 T3 Text 18: to evaluate the usefulness of text; Y2 T3 Text 19: to make simple notes from non-fiction texts.

Background
The internet can provide information on all sorts of subjects. However, it is important that children learn to assess the value of the information that they find and to use it effectively to answer questions. This activity aims to help the children begin to learn how to use the internet purposefully and efficiently. Check the websites to be used carefully before you begin, so that you can guide the children through the web pages and you know the information they contain.

Introduction
● Explain to the children that they are going to find out more about Remembrance Day from books and the internet.
● Ask the children what they can learn about Remembrance Day from books and the internet. Why do people put information about it on the internet? How is it useful?

Main teaching activity
● Look at pre-selected websites on a large computer screen or whiteboard during a whole-class session.
● Discuss and explain what the pages show. Encourage the children to ask and answer questions about what they see.
● On the board, write the headings: *What we want to know* and *What we found out*. Ask the children for a list of questions that they would like to find out about Remembrance Day. Write and number each question under the first heading.
● Tell the children that they will be recording their own answers on a sheet of paper or in their book. Demonstrate and support the children in recording, either in words or pictures, one or two examples. Write the answers under the second heading.
● Organise the children to work in pairs to record their answers, and encourage them to add questions of their own.

Plenary
● Discuss the children's answers and fill in the chart on the board, adding any additional questions and answers.
● Talk about the value of the internet as a source for finding out about the past, but remind the children of the dangers of using it, for example, finding a lot of irrelevant material, finding things that are not suitable for use in school, or by children.

Differentiation
Support less able writers when completing their answers or organise the children to work in mixed-ability pairs. It may be helpful to prepare sheets with a writing framework inlcuding the headings above.

Creating a play

Objectives
● To communicate their knowledge of history through role play.

Vocabulary
rifle, trench, mud, bomb

Resources
Simple props and scenery, such as a picture of a broken tree without leaves, a dark sky lit up by an explosion, broken fences, the inside of a trench; the photocopiable sheet 'A poem from the First World War' on page 159, or a suitable poem or prose extract of your choice.

Links
NC English KS1: En1 (1) to speak clearly and with confidence; (2) to listen and respond to others; (4) to participate in a range of drama activities.

Background
This lesson provides an opportunity for the children to revise and show what they have learned about the experiences of soldiers during the First World War. It also provides teachers and helpers an opportunity to assess the children's understanding of the historical knowledge, skills and understanding they have acquired in the course of the topic.

Introduction
● Explain to the class that they are going to make a play about wartime.
● Read a suitable war poem (such as 'Bombardment' on the photocopiable sheet on page 159) to the children. Alternatively use a prose extract, such as a piece from a first-hand account of war.

Main teaching activity
● Work with the children to set up a small corner of the classroom as a backdrop to the scene. You can encourage the children to make props and scenery as time allows, or you can provide much of the scene for them and just ask them to help you arrange the various pieces in place.
● Talk about what is happening in the poem or diary extract that you have read to the children. List their ideas on the board.
● Discuss with the children what they need to show if they are going to do a play or scene about wartime. Again, list these ideas on the board and develop them with the children.
● Divide the children into groups and assign each group one of the ideas to mime in the role play, so that some of the children are eating, some talking, some are in battle and some are sleeping.
● Choose one child to be the 'writer'. Ask this child to mime writing during the role play and, at the end, to stand up and read the poem, or the diary extract.
● Let the children practise and rehearse the scene, making alterations and improvements along the way. Are there any other props or scenery that would make the mime more effective?

Plenary
● Perform the scene, either as part of a class assembly or as part of a presentation of their work on the topic to another class.

Differentiation
Provide extra support for the less able children in their group activities or, alternatively, ensure that the children work in mixed-ability groups, so that the less able children are supported by their peers. Encourage older or more able children to extend the role play by adding other ideas to the mime.

An assembly for Remembrance Day

Objectives
● To communicate their knowledge of history in a variety of ways.

Vocabulary
Remembrance Day, poppy, First World War, Second World War

Resources
Stories, accounts and poems that the children have either used or created themselves; pictures, charts, role play and dramatic scenes they have created.

Background
An assembly allows the children to show what they have learned about the experiences of soldiers during the First World War, the purpose of Remembrance Day, and memories. It also provides teachers an opportunity to reward and value children's work and the historical knowledge, skills and understanding they have acquired.

Introduction
● Explain to the class that, on or near Remembrance Day, they will be leading an assembly about it.
● Tell the children that they will be holding up their work and saying a few words about it in turn. They will be telling the stories and reading the poems they have heard and written themselves. Those with stories can read them out to the audience.
● Recap that Remembrance Day is about remembering, and that, while the children are remembering what they have learned, they are also remembering the people who have died in wars.

Main teaching activity
● Group the children to plan how they will present different aspects of their work together, for example, an explanation of why we wear poppies on Remembrance Day; pictures and paintings of poppies and poppy fields; stories and poems, such as those written by soldiers who were in the war; short dramatic scenes; timelines of events; work they have completed about memories and so on.
● Rehearse the assembly in the room where it is to take place - this will give the children confidence.
● Support the children as necessary before and during the assembly, so that all the children are able to learn and achieve something from taking part in the assembly.
● Make sure that the assembly is instructive and interesting for the audience as well as enjoyable for the children taking part.

Plenary
● Following the assembly, invite any visitors to come into the classroom to look at the work produced over the course of the topic. Encourage the children to talk about what they have learned.

Differentiation
Organise the presentations appropriately according to the different ages and abilities within the class, for example, the more able children could read stories or poems, while the less able children could show pictures they have made, saying a few words about them. Less confident children could be encouraged to work within a group.

Links
NC English KS1: En1 (1) to speak clearly and with confidence; (2) to listen and respond to others; (8d) speaking to different people; (11b) presenting drama and stories to others.

Making your own poppy

◼ Colour and cut out these poppy petals, leaf and centre to make your own poppy.

◀**SCHOLASTIC**

Remembering the Second World War

◄ Write one question that you would like to ask a visitor about the Second World War.

What we found out

Our questions

A soldier's account

25th September 1915: Battle of Loos. I am on guard and about three in the morning the artillery bombardment started and the Boches reply in earnest. The noise of firing guns and exploding shells become one continuous and deafening crash. At 10.15 we get the order to get on top and we scrambled out of the trench and moved forward. The battle is in full-swing. Some wounded tell us that five lines of trenches have been taken. We got well past the German front line and then we saw the full horrors of war. We suddenly come under heavy machine gun fire. What a sight, dozens of men falling. Bob George was running beside me, and he suddenly goes over with a long drawn sigh. A Jock near me mutters 'killed', but somehow I did not realise that my best chum had gone under. We wavered and the officer shouts 'come on men' and we go on.

This is a diary account by 21-year-old George Smith from East Grinstead, West Sussex.

© The Royal Engineers Library, Chatham

◣SCHOLASTIC

A poem from the First World War

Bombardment

Four days the earth was rent and torn
By bursting steel,
The houses fell about us;
Three nights we dared not sleep,
Sweating, and listening for the imminent crash

Which meant our death.
The fourth night every man,
Nerve-tortured, racked to exhaustion,
Slept, muttering and twitching,
While the shells crashed overhead.

The fifth day there came a hush;
We left our holes
And looked above the wreckage of the earth
To where the white clouds moved in silent lines
Across the untroubled blue.

Richard Aldington

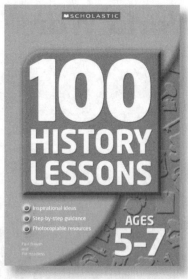
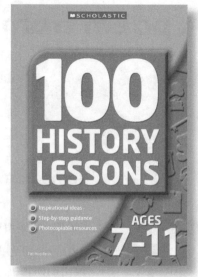